How To Be Unbothered:
A Guide to Non-Reactiveness, Perspective, and Protecting Your Peace

by Nick Trenton

www.NickTrenton.com

Table of Contents

INTRODUCTION — 5

SECTION 1: BREAKING THE CHAINS OF REACTIVITY — 13

REFRAME INSULTS: MASTER YOUR PERCEPTION — 13
REDUCE COMMITMENTS: PROTECT YOUR PEACE OF MIND — 23
THE "FILTER TEST" FOR EXTERNAL EXPECTATIONS — 31

SECTION 2: A RECIPE FOR A "GOOD LIFE" — 43

CHANGE YOUR PERSPECTIVE WITH PERMA: REAL GRATITUDE — 43
CULTIVATE FLOURISHING WITH PERMA: FIND YOUR FLOW — 52
STRENGTHEN YOUR RESILIENCE WITH PERMA: REACH OUT AND CONNECT — 62
BUILD LIFE SATISFACTION WITH PERMA: SET GOALS AND ACHIEVE THEM — 64
MEANING AND RESILIENCE — 73

SECTION 3: THE WISDOM OF THE STOICS — 79

CONTROL WHAT YOU CAN, LET GO OF WHAT YOU CAN'T — 79
PRACTICE NEGATIVE VISUALIZATION — 87

Respond With Indifference: Starve Negativity of Power   96

SECTION 4: PEACE IS SIMPLICITY   109

Practice Calming Micro-Activities   109
Scale Down Digital Noise   115
Simplify Decision-Making to Reduce Stress   123

SECTION 5: RECONCILE YOURSELF WITH FEAR   133

Face Panic Instead of Avoiding It   133
Talk to Panic: Reframe Fear Through Dialogue   145
Embodied Poise: Stand Calm to Feel Calm   153
Stand Without Crutches   160

SECTION 6: BECOME UNBAITABLE   173

Handle Criticism With Logic, Not Emotion   173
Thought Labeling: Observe, Don't Get Hooked   185
Emotional Distancing: Become a Witness, Not a Reactor   194

CONCLUSION   203

Introduction

So, what's gotten on your nerves today?

Maybe it was the stupid noise outside your window that woke you up this morning.

Maybe some jerk was mean to you for no reason and now you can't stop arguing with him in your head.

Maybe you're secretly troubled by that weird health gripe that just won't go away.

Maybe you spent hours doomscrolling last night and now you're annoyed because your head hurts. And also the world appears to be ending.

Maybe that project at work is taking way longer than it should, you bought the wrong cat food again, and you forget to cancel that trial subscription, so you've just lost $80 you doubt you'll ever see again.

Oh, and by the way, did you see that stinking review a customer left you?

Argh! Life is *stressful*.

Is it because you're an overthinker? Is all this tension because you're anxious or depressed or traumatized or burnt out?

Nope. In this book, we're going to be exploring **the deeper phenomenon beneath all these problems: your reactivity.**

Very simply, you're bothered.

You're *disturbed*.

Something has come along and interrupted your flow, rudely disconnected you from your reality, broken your concentration, or thrown you off kilter.

You're like a tightrope walker thrashing from side to side just before they lose balance and fall. You're like a pond that breaks into choppy waves and ripples when a stone is thrown into it. You're like a plane someone has hijacked and detoured to some new destination.

Let's be honest: The world today feels like a triggered and triggering place. There's a lot to be bothered about! People everywhere are agitated, provoked, and riled up to fever pitch, but what can we do to unplug, unsubscribe, and step away?

This book attempts to answer that question.

In the chapters that follow, we'll be investigating proven methods for:

- Improving your emotional regulation
- Finding more stability, poise, and self-control in your life
- Connecting to a deep, inner stillness—even when things around you are crazy

In short, our goal is to **reduce reactivity** so that we become unflustered, cool, calm, and collected. Unbothered. No matter what.

When you master the art of being imperturbable, the world suddenly becomes clearer and more relaxed. Life smooths out and opens up before you.

- You feel more at ease and confident in who you are and what you're doing.
- You're more focused and less distractable.
- You're resilient and strong.
- You're calmer and more emotionally even.
- You're able to readily spot solutions and new opportunities.
- You're self-determined, meaning you set the frame, you control the narrative, and you hold your own. Easily.
- You live at your own pace, on your own terms, according to your own values... and people respect you for it.

Being unflappable is *not* about mere stress-management.

Rather, it's an attitude. An orientation to life. A kind of *poise*.

What's more, serene composure is about so more than just being relaxed or happy.

It's about self-ownership.

It's about adopting that firm, upright inner posture that announces, "I am master of myself."

And from that solid, powerful center flows a life that is full of intention and authority.

You act with more decisiveness and less waste. You're not ruffled by everyday disturbances and setbacks. You're slow to upset and quick to return to baseline, choosing always to prioritize your purpose… and let go of the rest.

With the techniques and approaches we will discuss in this book, you will become a tightrope walker who only has eyes for the rope, a pond that quickly returns to stillness, and a plane that flies *directly* to its destination, no matter who or what might try to divert you.

In short, you stop being someone the world pushes around, and start standing firm in yourself.

But wait! Being unbothered is *not* about making yourself callous, aloof, or hard-hearted. It's got nothing to do with shutting down your empathy or pretending not to care (when you really, really do).

Our goal is not to be hyperrational or emotionally neutered, and we're not trying to escape into lofty detachment, refusing to engage at all.

Brittle things break before they bend. To state it differently, true strength and resilience may look a lot more flexible and accommodating than you may first imagine. Thriving sometimes looks like adjusting, adapting, bending around circumstances—this the heart of **emotional regulation**, and it's one of life's unappreciated superpowers.

There is strength in flow.

We can learn to be unbreakable in the way that a river is unbreakable.

In these pages, we'll be exploring how to:

- **Lower emotional reactivity.** We'll take a closer look at the power of perception, and how to protect our peace of mind by managing life's demands on our time, attention, and energy. We'll learn the magic of discernment: i.e., filtering out the good and letting go of the rest!
- **Create a life of flourishing.** What makes a life worth living? We'll carefully investigate the five main ingredients and how you can start living with more joy, connection, meaning, satisfaction, and flow—no matter what life throws your way.

- **Master the art of self-management.** Being cool and calm is never an accident. It's a conscious choice, a life habit, and a skill that follows a surprisingly simple formula. We'll unpack that formula and find ways to put this ancient law of serenity into practice today.
- **Trim away the fluff.** There are things in your life right now that are weighing you down, distracting you, and cluttering up your peace. We'll discover straightforward ways to cut the noise and simplify.
- **Overcome your fears.** Fear is a fact of life. With the right mindset, however, we can face it with real courage and stand firm in those things that we know matter more.
- **Stay steady in an unsteady world.** You can be an island of stillness in the chaos. We find ways to become unbaitable, un-hookable, and immune to threat and emotional manipulation—especially the kinds we might subject ourselves to!

If any of that sounds like it may make your life easier, then take heart: *Anyone* can learn to be less reactive, to re-anchor in their purpose, and to stand strong against those forces that seek to ruffle, displace, or dislodge us.

Now matter how stressed or unsteady you feel right now, you *can* learn to be unbothered.

The first step? Simply decide that this is what you'll do.

Set a firm intention.

Ready? Then we'll proceed.

All you'll need from here on out is a little patience, an open mind, and a willingness to try something new.

Let's dive in!

Section 1: Breaking the Chains of Reactivity

"Reactivity is enslavement. Responsibility is freedom. When you are able to create yourself the way you want, you can create your life the way you want as well. Your outer life may not be a hundred percent in your control, but your inner life always will."

- Sadhguru

Reframe Insults: Master Your Perception

Imagine that you're out walking one day when an arrow comes whizzing through the air and lands squarely in the middle of your chest.

The pain is *instant*.

Someone is attacking you, you've been shot, and it hurts like hell.

You respond immediately with anger, fear, defensiveness… or a messy mix of all three.

Insults, criticisms, and disapproving comments can *feel* like this arrow wound feels. They feel like attacks, and it feels like you have no choice but to respond with pain and anger.

But here's the trick: Though it *feels* this way, it actually isn't this way. **Insults are not actual attacks (like being shot by an arrow) but *potential* attacks.**

Allow me to explain.

Imagine that there is nobody out walking one day, and the arrow is shot into… an empty space.

Who cares, right?

There is no chest to hit, no pain, no anger, no fear.

That's because an arrow fired at nothing means nothing.

In order for an arrow attack to occur, you need an arrow, you need someone to shoot it… and *you also need a victim*. If the victim doesn't show up? The attack has nowhere to land.

"Taking offense" is like showing up to get shot by that arrow. It's *being there*, emotionally and mentally.

If you don't even register an insult, if you ignore it, if you withdraw your attention and fail to react, who is present to be insulted?

Here is where your power lies. **You can choose your reaction.**

You can choose *not* to be the place where the arrow lands. (Hint: People soon get bored of firing arrows that never find a target).

When you're insulted, it can feel like you're instantly wounded... but this pain is partly an illusion. The hurt is not just from the arrow, but your perception of that arrow. Fail to participate in that pain, and there isn't any.

An insult ignored is like fire without oxygen.

Like a joke without a punchline.

Like a bomb with the fuse cut off.

In other words, **by ignoring an insult you deprive it of all its significance and power.**

However, if you react, you feed it that oxygen. You supply the fuel and the punchline, you give the bomb its fuse, and you light it. An insult is a half-formed thing that someone sets down. By picking it up again, you make it a fully formed thing. Essentially, it's about *agreement*. By picking up an insult that somebody sets down, you are saying:

- I agree that this opinion has value and matters—even more than my own opinion, or my peace of mind
- I agree that I am defined by other people's comments and judgments
- I agree that I am insecure and unstable in my own identity

- I agree that people's careless or hurtful words are a genuine threat to me
- I agree that other people are allowed to steer me, command my attention, and control my state of mind

Reacting with pain and indignation feels automatic and even (if we're honest) a little thrilling. Nobody wants to be disrespected, right? But the truth is, every time you rise to react in this way, *you agree to all of the above.*

Knee-jerk anger is expensive:

- It costs you your serenity.
- It costs you your clarity of thought.
- It clouds your judgment.
- It poisons your relationships.
- It tempts you towards reckless retaliation.

Worst of all? Anger places you squarely into the hands of others. It's like handing them a string and giving them permission to pull it any time they want to make you jump, like a puppet.

Unkind words are *not* arrows. They don't pierce our flesh without our permission.

Words are just symbols, and they require *us* to interpret and understand them.

The great Stoic Seneca said that **"We suffer more in imagination than in reality."**

What did he mean? Somebody says a harsh word and, without knowing it, we actually *elaborate* on that insult in our own minds, extending it, making it deeper and richer and more painful in our own minds. We nurse that hurt.

It's worth saying again: **We hurt ourselves with our own perception and interpretation of others' words.**

However, if you choose not to do any of this, then the other person's words are revealed to be what they were all along: symbols.

Sounds.

Someone just opened their mouth and a sound came out.

The air waves vibrated a little, then it was over.

They typed a few keys on a keyboard and pixels appeared on a screen. Then time moved on and the next thing came along. That's it.

That's all that happened.

Do you want to make it more than that?

Three Practical Ways to be Less Reactive

Pause Before Reacting

The brilliant author and Holocaust survivor Viktor Frankl once famously said,

> *"Between stimulus and response there is a space. In that space is our power to choose*

> *our response. In our response lies our growth and our freedom."*

It's hard to put it more succinctly than that.

Being unbothered is simply about finding that space. Skipping that beat. Even if it's only a little window of a few seconds, that breathing space will help remind you of the immense power you hold in that moment.

You shift your perspective, you remember your autonomy, and you claim your right to choose. All of this protects you from careless impulse.

Try this: The next time you feel that little sting of a verbal arrow, pause.

JUST STOP.

Take a breath.

Mentally say to yourself, "What happens next is up to me."

Find your center and your stillness.

The really great thing? Not only do you get to choose your reaction, but you also get to choose whether you respond at all. That may seem like an impossibility sometimes, but I encourage you to push yourself and try it the next time you feel slighted or annoyed.

Quietly watch yourself sailing right past that indignation and anger. See it as a bus headed in that direction—a bus you see come and go, that you simply choose to not board.

Example 1: A colleague snaps at you during a meeting. Your first impulse is to snap back and put them in their place. But you stop. You take a breath. You think, "Huh, they're probably stressed about something else." Then you actively disentangle those little fingers of anger off your heart, and move swiftly on.

Example 2: Some random stranger leaves a hurtful comment on your social media post. You read it, feel the sting, feel the heat, *then stop*. You watch yourself choose to not care. You watch yourself find that space. You think, "That person obviously needs to do that to feel better about themselves, but I don't really care about the deeper reason why. Their problem, not mine."

You delete the comment, not just from social media, but also from your mind.

Label Negativity as "Noise"
If you're walking down the sidewalk and encounter a muddy puddle, what do you do?

Walk around it, probably.

If a fly starts buzzing around your head, what do you do?

Shoo it away, probably.

If you see a rotten apple mixed in with the good ones at the supermarket, what do you do?

Choose a good one and avoid the rotten one, probably.

Sure, these things are annoying, unwanted, and unpleasant. But they're also kind of irrelevant, right?

You just mentally file them as unimportant, slightly adjust your path around them and carry on living the life you were living before you knew they even existed.

Makes sense, so why don't we do the same when we encounter rude, negative, or hostile people?

A rude person's comment is exactly like a dirty puddle, a buzzing fly, or a rotten apple—annoying, but not really relevant. Certainly not worth getting bothered about!

Think in terms of **signal** and **noise**.

The meaning, value, and purpose of life? That's your signal. That's what you pay attention to. That's your path, your mission, and your intention. That's where your energy and focus belongs.

Everything else? That's noise. You might hear it and see it, but be sure to disregard it. It's not on the path, and it's not part of the mission.

Try this: Take a breath, find that gap, and tell yourself, "That's just noise."

You don't have to go to war, or engage, or argue, or get caught up. Just file it as unimportant and move on.

Example: That rude jerk was pretty hostile to you in traffic. But that's *his* bad mood, *his* life choice, *his* action. Why should it also be yours?

See it, shake it off, and move on.

So much of the random negativity we encounter in life is not even about us, but about other people's struggles. Remind yourself that you've probably lashed out before for the same reason, right?

Don't take it personally.

The puddle isn't making a claim about your worth as a human being, the rotten apple isn't rotting to spite you, and the fly doesn't have a vendetta against you specifically.

Reframe negativity and hostility as meaningless noise, and you can walk away from it. This is emotional freedom.

Respond Consciously

You may be wondering, "Wait, is it really wise to dismiss *every* piece of criticism I receive?"

Let's be real and admit that sometimes, there is a grain of truth in the criticism we receive, and sometimes we do affect the behavior we receive from others.

We need to:

- Genuinely reflect
- Carefully consider
- Be fiercely honest

The trick, of course, is that we can only do all of that when we are calm and non-reactive.

Try this: If something really stings, it's worth taking a moment to calm down first. Give your nervous system time to settle. Let things rest for a while—maybe sleep on it.

Then, sit with a journal and carefully look through the insult or criticism. Look at it like a forensic scientist or investigative journalist.

- What is really true here?
- Are you making any assumptions?
- Is there any insight to be gleaned from this?

Example: Someone critiques your work quite harshly, and it hurts. You give yourself a day or two for the steam to blow off, then ask yourself honestly if there's any truth in it. Then, you deliberately choose your reaction. You decide that although the other person was unnecessarily mean, and probably exaggerating, the truth is that you didn't really try as hard as you could have.

The "insult" is now neutralized—it becomes food for improvement.

Reduce Commitments: Protect Your Peace of Mind

In the previous chapter, we saw that other people's comments, judgments and insults do not necessarily have to impact our state of mind.

We can choose not to take on unnecessary pain or anger.

In the same way, **we can choose not to take on unnecessary *hurry*.**

When something or someone makes a demand on us, we are at liberty to decide how we respond. We can say yes. Or we can say no.

When people say things like…

- "I'm so busy!"
- "There's too much to do."
- "I have no choice, I have to…"
- "I have obligations."

…what they are really saying is:

- "I have allowed my peace of mind to be encroached upon. I have allowed people and things to eat away my time, energy, and peace."

Can you see the different between the two?

Saying, "There is so much that needs to be done," is **passive**. It gives all the power to the things that need to be done. These things, whatever they are, are the lord and master of your universe, and they determine what you do and how you do it.

To say, "I have *allowed* these things to intrude into my life" is **active**. It gives all the power to you.

When you can acknowledge that *you* are the one who is allowing certain things to make demands of you, then you empower yourself to also be the one to change things.

Life *will* make demands on you. But it is up to you whether you authorize those demands, fulfil them, or give them permission to stress you out.

One of the biggest sources of stress and overthinking? It's not the existence of demands. It's giving in to those demands when you shouldn't and don't want to.

It's being passive, not active.

Author of *The Art of Going Slow* Damon Zahariades (2024) explains that it's really up to us to manage our commitments, to budget our time and energy, and to proactively choose the pace of the life we want to live.

Importantly, we need to stop blaming whatever makes demands on us, and take a close look at the one acquiescing to those demands (that's us).

Choosing to do less, go more slowly, or say no is not laziness. It's intentionality.

When you are focused, you:

- Zoom in what matters (more signal, less noise)
- Lower your anxiety
- Stay resilient in the face of minor disruptions and aggravation

Hustle Culture says that success means pushing harder when you're floundering and overwhelmed. It says that we can vanquish stress by *increasing* the demands we entertain.

You already know that this doesn't work, right?

What *does* work is pausing, reorienting towards what actually matters to you, and being honest about your hard limits.

All the time, energy, attention and life force that you're leaking into things that don't matter can be more actively channeled into the things that do matter—force, hustle, and depletion not required.

Three Practical Ways to Guard Your Serenity

Do a "Yes Audit" Once a Week

It may seem strange, but you may not even be aware of the biggest "stress leaks" in your life right now.

Think of it this way: It's the automatic and unconscious "yes" habits that are the most damaging, because you don't even realize that you have the option to say no to these things.

We all have:

- Limited time
- Limited energy
- Limited attention
- Limited resources

That seems like the most obvious statement you could possibly make, right? And yet many of us carry on in life as though we don't really believe it's true.

We say yes as though our time, energy, attention, and resources truly are infinite.

Try this: Look backward at the week just gone. Day by day, make a list of everything that you said yes to.

Maybe that was an additional work task, a favor for a friend, a last-minute social invitation, a request from a neighbor, a plea to support a local charity, even little things like a piece of junk mail that came through the letterbox or a random call from your mother in the middle of a busy workday.

Now, put on neutral, curious eyes and go through each item on your list:

- Did this thing drain or energize you?
- Was this thing really your responsibility?
- Is this something you genuinely care about?
- Did this thing add value or will it add value in the future somehow?
- Did you even want to do this thing?

Your goal is not to chip away at every responsibility and obligation until you do nothing for anyone ever. There will absolutely be things on your list that matter, and that are worth doing, even if they cost you.

That said, you're trying to find what *doesn't* fit those criteria.

What did you say yes to out of fear, obligation, shame, or guilt?

What did you say yes to out of pride, vanity, or a desire to be needed?

What did you say yes to out of ignorance, habit, or confusion?

Mark those things that you want to play differently next time round. Make a commitment to yourself that you will answer "no" the next time this demand rears its head.

Every no you say to an unnecessary commitment is a *yes* you can say to something else that genuinely enriches your life.

Use the Pause Rule Before Saying Yes

Even a question or a request can be thought of as a demand.

When someone asks something, we can feel compelled to respond as quickly as possible.

But here's a liberating thought: **A request doesn't impose anything on you at all.**

It's just a question.

You are not required to respond immediately. You don't have to instantly jump to attention. People can make requests, but their request doesn't automatically entitle them to a particular response, *nor the speed of that response.*

- Are they in a hurry? It doesn't mean you have to be in a hurry.
- Are they really stressed out about it? It doesn't mean you have to be, too.
- Are they certain about the response you owe them? It doesn't mean you have to agree!

In other words, just take a minute. Rushing to respond often leads to overcommitment. Which then leads to resentment.

Try this: Has someone caught you off guard with a spontaneous request or demand? Pause and take a breath. Then ask for time. Easy.

- "Hey, can I get back to you on that?"

- "I'll have to check my calendar first, though."
- "Can I think it over and let you know tomorrow morning?"

For those people pleasers in our midst, a sudden request can catch you on the back foot and have you saying yes before you know what's happening. However, if you take the time to practice and rehearse responses like those above, then you can gain the psychological relief of a quick response without overcommitting yourself.

Smile. Be polite. But be firm.

It's OK to need time to think, and it's not rude to ask for it.

Example 1: Your next-door neighbor catches you on your way to work one morning and asks if you'll watch their dog while they're away over the weekend. You smile, and politely say, "Oh, cool, I love Bingo. But let me double check my schedule and see if I'm actually around this weekend!"

Example 2: Your mother calls you up during a busy workday. You quickly determine whether it's an emergency or not, and when you confirm that it isn't, you say, "Mom, I'm just busy with something right now. How about I call you back later this evening at 7?"

(Hint: Emails, phone calls, and text messages are requests, not non-negotiable orders. You don't necessarily *have to* answer every single one, and if you do, remember that you also have a say over how that conversation unfolds, and how long it lasts).

Replace One Commitment With Self-Care

Bosses can be unreasonable, charity workers (and mothers!) can lay on the guilt, and friends can subtly pile on the peer pressure and expectations. Sometimes, it really does feel like everyone wants a piece of you.

But the truth is that **we cannot blame other people for our lack of peace, our stress levels, or our failure to pursue our priorities.**

Those things are our responsibility.

When you stop blaming others for a life that feels rushed, exhausting, or overburdened, then you allow yourself to take charge of making good decisions for yourself.

Are your time, energy, and attention worth anything to you? Then protect them.

Does your peace matter? What about your values, your goals, and your priorities? Nobody else will defend those things on your behalf.

Don't be a martyr.

Don't expect that people will be impressed with your sacrifice or that you will one day be rewarded for eternally putting yourself last.

Instead, actively convert overcommitment and over responsibility into self-care.

Try this: Each time you remove a draining obligation, make a habit of swapping it out for something calming or restorative.

Example: You could waste a lot of time grumbling that a close friend keeps asking you to lend them money and give them lifts. You may feel unappreciated, taken for granted, and frustrated. But all the same you keep saying yes… then blame them for having asked.

Instead, say no.

That's it. Just no.

How can they take your limits and boundaries seriously if *you* don't? Stop expecting them to appreciate you and do something to appreciate yourself. Take that time and money and go out for a piece of cake, take a nice walk, or treat yourself to a little something you've had your eye on.

The "Filter Test" for External Expectations

You know how that random email lands in your Inbox, loudly declaring that it's **URGENT**?

We all know it really isn't urgent.

A key insight: Not everything that claims to be important, or indeed feels important, actually *is*.

The world is full of outright demands on our attention but also unspoken, implicit expectations about where our time and energy ought to be going. We may even internalize these demands and expectations so that we hold ourselves hostage to unconscious "shoulds" and "musts."

One form of reactivity that many of us have been trained in—and indeed continue to train ourselves in—is the habit of responding to everything *indiscriminately*.

We appraise every incoming stimulus, every demand on us, and every expectation as though they were all on the same level. We give all triggers equal airtime, granting them equal claim on our attention and energy.

Everything claims to be important and urgent, but only some things are.

How can you tell the difference? Clearly, relying on your emotional response alone won't get you very far.

One way to reduce reactivity is to gain a little **psychological distance** (more on that later) and guard your serenity by consciously choosing how to perceive and frame your experiences.

Another way is **temporal distancing,** i.e., putting a little *time* between you and a stimulus. Simply, it's reappraising the present from a future perspective.

What does that look like?

Well, one underappreciated way to filter out noise is to just "wait and see."

If something's genuinely important, then the mere passage of time will confirm it.

However, have you ever been caught up in a big life drama only to watch it fizzle completely within a few days? Have you ever struggled to solve a major problem only for it to just resolve itself?

Besides waiting for time to literally move on, a more dependable approach may be to ***imagine the passage of time. From within that perspective*, reappraise just how urgent and important something really is. Then respond accordingly.**

Panic and reactivity are RIGHT HERE RIGHT NOW phenomena:

- Do you feel pressured, rushed, or somehow coerced by a shortage of time?
- Do you feel like you're being pushed a little?
- Do you feel almost like you're being held hostage?

This could signal that you're in a reactive, dependent, and triggered frame of mind. Rushing and panic are a sign you're being manipulated by fear—either your own or other people's.

Temporal distancing puts a check on that fear.

Three Practical Ways to Practice Temporal Distancing

The 5-Year Filter Test

Try this: When something emerges in your field of awareness and claims to be urgent and important, don't automatically take its word for it. Remember that not everything demanding your attention deserves it, and not everything that says it's urgent is telling the truth. Indeed, it may be really urgent... for someone else, though, not for you.

When something is bothering you, upsetting your balance, or throwing you into a panic, pause, and pass it through a filter:

- Will this matter in a month?
- Will this matter in a year?
- Will this matter in five years?
- At the end of my life, when I'm on my deathbed and looking back at it all, will I still care about this thing or even remember it?

If not, there's a good chance this thing is not really, truly important.

The things that will matter in a year or five years or for the rest of your life tend to be the big things—the things that deserve your full, focused attention and all the energy you can muster.

Let's not lie to ourselves—there *are* things that are this serious and this important.

Decisions that might lead to you contracting a life-threatening disease, getting divorced, going to prison, inheriting millions, moving to a different country, or having a child—these are the kinds of things that have earned the right to your full and immediate attention.

But what about…

- A rude comment online?
- A bad haircut?
- A $20 parking fine?
- A lost umbrella?
- A stubbed toe?

These things matter *a little*. But they aren't truly significant in the grand scheme of life.

There is a sting there, no doubt. But for most everyday disturbances, **our reaction often lasts longer than the trigger itself**. With the passage of time each of these things will vanish into nothingness. If we're honest, even a few weeks is sometimes enough to permanently erase from our minds the memory that we were ever bothered in the first place.

So why get bothered in the first place?

Categorize Reactions
Be selective about where your attention goes.

Recognize that you have the right and the ability to moderate your response according to the stimulus.

Try this: Mentally sort your concerns according to two factors:

1. Urgency
2. Importance

When you can correctly understand what a thing is, you can more accurately identify your best response to it. This frees up your mental bandwidth and releases you from any unnecessary tension and fluster.

- Urgent – These things are genuinely time dependent. The deadline is Tuesday, for example. A plane is taking off at a fixed time, the sun is setting, the shop is closing.
- Important – These things are truly significant and matter given your goals, values, and purpose. Your wedding day, for example, is a pretty big deal.

We can combine these two factors to create *four different categories* to sift through any of life's emergent demands or expectations:

- Urgent and important
- This thing matters, *and* there's a time limit.
- These are the things that legitimately deserve your attention and energy.
- Example: You need to get to the church at 10 a.m. sharp for your wedding.

- Important but not urgent
- These things align with your goals and values, but there isn't any immediate rush to do them.
- These things deserve your *consistent* and habitual energy, attention, and focus.
- Example: A good diet, exercise, and proper sleep schedule are important for longevity and wellbeing—but there's no deadline as such; long-term, cumulative habits will take care of it.
- Urgent but not important
- There is a time limit, but it's for something trivial or relatively minor.
- These are things that should not be allowed to claim too much of your time, attention, or energy.
- Example: There's a "limited time offer" ending soon on a product you don't especially want or need.
- Not urgent and not important
- These things are neither time-bound nor significant in any way.
- Obviously, they don't deserve any of your time, energy, or attention. In fact, there's no need to respond at all except to briefly identify and dismiss.
- Example: A neighbor wants to gossip and complain about something that's firmly in the past, which doesn't concern you, and which involves people you've never met nor will ever meet.

These categories are listed in order, with the most decisive factor being importance.

1. If it's truly important, engage.
2. Of the things that aren't important, prioritize those things that are more urgent—if you choose to engage at all, that is.

With just these two rules, you order and prioritize your own responses, avoid wasting energy, and give yourself informed permission to ignore what is simply not relevant.

A few points to remember:

- **Gain perspective**. If you're having difficulty identifying the seriousness of a trigger or demand, zoom out. Project yourself into the future. Something may feel urgent and important right now, but check in with your future self—will this thing *continue* to feel important as time goes on?
- **"Important" is a subjective appraisal**. We decide what matters to us according to our values, principles, and the goals we're trying to achieve. We don't have to agree with others about what is or isn't important. Be careful: Just because something is urgent and important to someone else, doesn't automatically make it so for *us*.
- **Remember your limits.** In life we have a limited amount of energy and a limited amount of time. When you feel burdened by guilt, obligation, shame, or the fear of regret,

remember that you don't have an unlimited budget. It may seem extreme, but the "deathbed test" will remind you that when all is said and done, there are some things that you are going to be glad to have done. *Don't let trivialities in the present take away from those things.*

Calm-Check Reminder

Of course, the above methods are *intellectual* strategies—they help us sort through things rationally and practically.

That's only half of the problem, though. The other half? We need to *emotionally* let go of the things we know are not relevant on an intellectual level.

There's no point agreeing with yourself that something is ignorable and irrelevant if you proceed to stress about it anyway.

Try this: Write a small cue like **"Filter → Let Go"** in your notebook, or create a little sign or sticky that you can place somewhere prominent and visible. Near a workstation or on a computer is a good idea, but you can also leave a reminder on your phone screen so that you see it every time you pick it up to scroll.

1. Is this important?
2. Is this urgent?
3. If no, let go.

Take a deep breath, relax, and visualize this thing drifting away from you. It's not yours. It's not about you. You don't need it, and it doesn't need you.

You're letting go of something that doesn't bring value to your life. That's a good thing!

In fact, there's no need to get too hung up on letting go if you can **immediately redirect your attention and energy to what *is* important and urgent.**

Just keep anchoring yourself in these three steps: filter, let go, redirect.

If your usual mode has been just one step (react!) then it will take some time to slow down and respond in a more deliberate way.

One final reminder: Stress, angst, rage, fear, despair, or doubt are never actually required, *even if* something is important and urgent. Being emotionally triggered is not required in order to care, pay attention, or solve a problem.

In short: Don't be bothered by irrelevant things… but don't be bothered by relevant things, either!

Summary:

- Insults are not actual attacks, but potential ones—your perception decides whether you will be a victim or not. We always have the power to choose our reaction. Ignoring

insults drains them of their power and significance over us.
- To be less reactive, find a little space and pause before reacting. Label negativity as unimportant noise and navigate around it. Reflect honestly to find any grain of truth.
- Actively claim your power and responsibility to decide how to respond to demands on your time, energy, or attention. Intentionally choose your pace and your focus.
- Do a regular "yes audit" to reappraise your commitments. Pause before acquiescing to demands, or politely ask for more time to decide. Where possible, replace a draining overcommitment with an act of replenishing self-care.
- Use temporal distancing to filter out the truly important from the unimportant. Carefully categorize events according to their urgency and importance.
- Consciously give your energy, effort, and attention to your priorities: those things that are important and urgent. Filter out the rest, then let go of what is irrelevant. Important or not, however, don't let it bother you!

Section 2: A Recipe for a "Good Life"

"People who flourish make a decision to flourish. They point themselves toward joy."

- Frank Bruni

Change Your Perspective with PERMA: Real Gratitude

In his 2012 book *Flourish: A Visionary New Understanding of Happiness and Well-Being*, American psychologist and author Martin Seligman explains a new model of mental health which he calls "positive psychology."

Don't let the name confuse you—positive psychology is not about being or feeling positive; instead, it's about **where we put our focus when we're attempting to live well.**

Traditional psychology models explore:

- Dysfunction
- Mental illness
- Deficiencies
- Diagnoses
- Problems

This is not unlike traditional medicine, which concerns itself with diseases, disorders, and impairments of function. The goal here is to remove the negative.

Positive psychology, however, isn't just concerned with what is lacking or what is broken. Positive psychology's claim is that **health is more than the absence of disease**. Instead, it tries to answer the question, "What does a human being look like when they're happy, thriving, and flourishing?"

Positive psychology is interested in…

- Healthy traits and qualities
- Strengths and virtues
- The nature of a good character
- Meaning and purpose
- Happiness and wellbeing
- Optimal functioning
- Relationships, community, and engagement

We can think of the difference between traditional and positive psychology as follows: **one is problem-focused, while the other is solution-focused.**

One asks, "What's going wrong here?"

The other asks, "What's going *right* here?"

Now, with all this mind, we can approach the broader question, "How can we be unbothered?" or **"How can we be more resilient?"**

The traditional answer might be "We can learn to better cope with stress, anxiety, and negativity in life."

But what might the positive psychology answer look like? "We can find ways to nourish and strengthen our innate positive traits, and cultivate a life that is richer, more connected, and more meaningful."

Big difference, right?

As Frank Bruni tells us, the good life is not just turning away from negativity, but "pointing towards joy."

Seligman proposed 5 ingredients for the happy, fulfilled life, expressed in his acronym **PERMA**:

- **P**ositive emotion
- **E**ngagement
- **R**elationships
- **M**eaning
- **A**ccomplishment

In the chapters that follow, we'll explore these building blocks one by one. For now, we simply need to understand the basic perspective switch that Seligman is inviting us to make.

For him, it's not enough to just relieve suffering or reduce stress; a good life is about challenging yourself to get the most out of life, and to *live well.*

Being a healthy, fulfilled human is about so much more than just being "happy." We need meaning, challenge, and rich relationships. We need hope, goals, and a chance to contribute to the world.

Make the switch:

- Withdraw focus from the negative, lack, weakness, dysfunction, or disorder.
- Invest focus into the positive, strengths, virtues, blessings, value, meaning, and purpose.

Positive emotions will result. One powerful way to make this switch? **Gratitude**.

Three Practical Ways to Be More Grateful

The practice of keeping a "gratitude journal" is recommended occasionally in self-help literature, but usually without much of an explanation for *why* we are attempting to feel so grateful in the first place. What's so special about thankfulness?

By now, you might guess some possible answers:

- **Being thankful helps us switch from a negative to a positive focus**. Remember, this is NOT about making yourself think of positive things. Instead, "positive" describes the quality of our focus. It's about finding health by *amplifying what's already working*, rather than removing disease by

addressing everything that's wrong or lacking.
- **Being thankful is a powerful antidote to anxiety**. While anxiety narrows focus, gratitude widens it again, and allows us to perceive more things, and to perceive them more accurately.
- **Being thankful doesn't just feel good, but it's also pretty smart.** Adopting an optimistic, open, and explorative frame of mind means you're more likely to identify opportunities and solutions to your problems.

Important: These benefits come from the genuine state of mind associated with appreciation, optimism, joy, and open-mindedness—*not* from merely listing out things you know you "should be grateful for."

Do a "Gratitude Rep"

The trouble with gratitude journals? They can quickly become automatic. A going-through-the-motions kind of thing.

Try this: Instead of thinking of various nice things you experienced today, *actively generate warm, appreciative feelings*, in real time.

This is not an intellectual exercise.

You're not making a list.

Instead, think of it as a gratitude gym—a place you go to practice and get good at holding and embodying a sincerely grateful attitude. You are training your conscious awareness, and teaching it where to put its focus, i.e., on all those good things that already exist all around you.

You are practicing the feeling of joy—not abstractly listing out things that theoretically make a person joyful.

That means you should *not*:

- Make things up
- Try too hard
- Pretend to feel grateful

Instead of mechanically listing out things like "The sun was shining," or "I got to eat an amazing jelly donut," pause and take a moment to really summon up and enjoy genuine feelings of thankfulness for that sunshine, and that donut.

Feel it.

Even if just for a moment, that little "rep" of gratitude in your gratitude gym is a powerful protectant against stress and anxiety.

Try a Mini-Gratitude Ritual
Remember that gratitude practice is about acknowledging all the blessings that are *already in your life* that you don't ordinarily notice.

What is called gratitude practice may be more accurately called a simple mindfulness exercise.

There are gifts and blessings all around you, right now, but your limited awareness of them means you don't truly acknowledge how lucky you are to have them.

Later, we will explore the counterintuitive technique of "negative visualization" to play with this idea even further. For now, we're just learning to build tiny moments of increased awareness of everything that's actually pretty good in life, right now, just as it is.

Instate a new ritual. Here are some ideas:

- Every time you get into bed, quickly think back over the day and identify a high point. Emotionally bring yourself back to those good feelings. Amplify them.
- **Make mealtimes a trigger for gratitude.** No matter who you are or what you're going through, the joy and privilege of simple food can be a powerful anchor back into gratitude for the small things—which are never that small when you focus on them! Pause before every meal to pray, be mindful, or simply say "thank you" mentally.
- **As you go through the day, be on the lookout for things to be grateful for.** The truth is that it doesn't really matter what these things are. What matters is your continued, hopeful, and expectant attention that is ready to perceive the good in things.

Every moment your brain is savoring the good, it's *not* dwelling on the bad.

Quit the Complaining Habit

You don't have to sit around, waiting to see whether life impresses you or not.

You don't have to passively appraise the usefulness of whatever comes your way, and rank experiences according to whether they meet some arbitrary threshold or not.

In fact, truly emotionally resilient people are **actively grateful**—independent of their actual circumstances. They go around with eyes willing to see beauty, abundance, and luck.

How different this is from the attitude of complaint!

When we complain, it can feel like all we're doing is stating our opinion about something objectively unpleasant in our world. But it's a trap! We're doing much more than this.

Complaining is being **passively ungrateful.**

It's going around with eyes that are only willing to see deficiency.

Complaining can mask deeply destructive attitudes of entitlement, apathy, and resentment. Moaning and grumbling is a habit that feels harmless (and even slightly enjoyable at times), but the cost is higher than you can imagine.

The next time you're tempted to complain, even (and especially) if you feel justified, remind yourself of what this shift in focus actually costs you:

- You're less resilient
- You're less creative
- You're less able to solve problems
- You're less receptive and open-minded
- You're less willing to take responsibility for your own actions
- Finally, let's be honest, you're more of a pain in the butt to be around!

Instead, **take every temptation to complain and turn it around.** Even if it feels a little artificial at first, deliberately try to find something that is going well for you and make a comment about that instead.

Is it too hot? Focus on how delicious your ice cream is.

Is the checkout line too long? Focus on how lucky it is that you have a few moments to draft that important email in your head.

Is life madly unfair? Focus on all those times you got something for nothing, when you totally didn't deserve it!

Cultivate Flourishing With PERMA: Find Your Flow

One way to shift to a positive focus is to actively cultivate gratitude—arguably one of the most powerful of the positive emotions.

Let's move on now to the **E in PERMA: Engagement**.

By *engagement*, Seligman is talking about the phenomenon that is elsewhere known as "flow" (Csikszentmihalyi, 1990). Engagement/flow can be understood as:

- Being completely absorbed and "at one" with a task or activity.
- Total focus, deep concentration, and "being in the moment" without any self-consciousness.
- Working at a level that is optimally balanced between challenge and reward (i.e., it's not so easy that it's boring, and it's not so challenging that you feel discouraged).

When you're in that flow zone, *you feel alive.*

You're working hard but you don't feel fatigued—only more engrossed.

This is well beyond merely feeling good or happy. This is not just recreation or pleasure; flow means being so immersed in your work that you lose track of time… or even lose track of self.

Deep engagement is a potent remedy for rushed multitasking, boredom, frustration, futility, and mindlessness. It's also a skill that emotionally mature and well-regulated people have mastered to a fine art.

So, which activities count as *engagement* or *flow* activities?

It turns out that this may not be the right question!

According to Bonaiuto et al. (2016), it's all about identifying those things that YOU are really passionate about—and that could be anything.

Try this: Ask yourself,

- What activities usually have me losing track of time?
- What tasks can I happily do for ages, without growing fatigued?
- What things do I find myself doing really well and with ease?
- What activities showcase my strengths and virtues the best?
- Where have I experienced flow before? What was I doing and how was I doing it?

Figure out which activities you already find natural flow with, and you have your answer: *Do more of those things!*

By bringing more of these activities into your life, you're bringing in more richness and depth.

You're connecting with life. You're interacting with your world in a full and generative way—and that is intrinsically rewarding.

But not every day can be filled with all the good stuff. What about your job? What about boring things like errands and housework?

The wonderful thing about cultivating more flow is that it's not necessarily about magnificent peak moments or sublime states of perfection—**to engage, all you really have to do is be present.**

Be in the moment.

When you do something, *do it*.

When you are somewhere, really *be there*.

Even mundane or familiar tasks can come alive when you stretch out in that moment with your full and total self.

Pay attention.

Perceive with all of your senses.

Watch, listen, observe.

Live this little moment of your life like nothing else exists beyond it. No distractions. Do this, and you may be surprised to find just how many little pockets of flow are packed into even the most ordinary day (Belitz & Lundstrom, 1998).

- *Washing dishes?* Pause and really sink into the sensation of warm water and bubbles on your skin. Isn't it amazing how much more you feel when you notice yourself feeling it?
- *Walking to the bus stop?* Just how fully can you inhabit this walking movement? Can you imagine that your full consciousness is in every limb, in every step?
- *The helpline put you on hold?* Don't just listen to the hold music; listen to *everything* happening around you. Contemplate that pause, that suspended moment held between one busyness and the next…

Flourishing can sometimes mean doing more, or doing better.

But sometimes it can just mean doing *what we're already doing* with more fullness and presence.

It's not what you do, as they say, it's the way that you do it. Every day is filled with activity. It's your choice how much you show up, and how fully involved you are with that activity.

Caveat: Engagement is not about happiness. It's about creating psychological reserves that make life feel rich and deep. These psychological reserves make you:

- Less reactive
- More resilient
- Better able to self-regulate
- Harder to disturb or upset

- More balanced
- More perceptive and aware
- Calmer

Think of engagement as a way to set down hooks or anchors into reality. The more firmly connected to real life you are, the harder it is to dislodge or distress you… and the less likely you are to disturb or distress *yourself*.

Three Practical Ways to Be More Engaged

Engage in One Flow Activity Each Day

You don't have to wait for inspiration to find you—go out and find it.

Choose one or two activities that you find most conducive to a flow state, and schedule in some time every day to immerse yourself. It can be:

- Writing or reading
- Drawing, doodling, painting, or making art
- Singing, dancing, or making music
- Cooking or baking
- Playing an engrossing and immersive game, alone or with others
- Vigorous exercise, sport, or an invigorating hike

Engagement resets your mind and recenters you. You feel inspired, rewarded, and *interested* in life—which is a fundamentally healthy and resilient state to be in. Staying actively connected to your world through engrossing activity is an effective moderator of everyday stress.

Ever gone to bed and thought, "Wow, I had a really good day today"? Chances are, what you had was a day of engagement and presence.

Learn to Stay in the Process
There is a strange kind of paradox built into the flow state: You are working towards a definite goal, yet somehow you are not focused on that goal at all.

What are you focused on? The process unfolding right in front of you.

Some people can have self-limiting but largely unconscious assumptions about "work" and "play" that hinder their ability to enjoy a flow state.

These beliefs go a little something like this:

> Play is fun, but work is… well, work is work, and you do it to get it done. It's not meant to be enjoyable. It's done purely for a purpose, and stops just as soon as that purpose has been fulfilled. If you're smart, you need to race to that finish line as quickly as possible. Why? So you can get back to what you *really* want to do… having fun!

Granted, this may be an oversimplification, but much of our culture is set up around this work vs. play distinction. The unspoken assumption is that work is a means to an end.

While this makes logical sense, the brain in a flow state actually operates in precisely the opposite way. When you are in flow:

- The boundaries between work and play dissolve. Play can be hard, and work can be fun.
- You enjoy the process of the activity, not just the outcome it leads to. You certainly care about the goal—sometimes intensely so—but what keeps you going is your continued fascination with each step that takes you closer.
- You are intrinsically motivated. In other words, you act not because someone will reward or incentivize you, but because you value the task for its own sake, or for a purpose you've determined independently.

Ironically, being too goal-oriented or obsessed with results can backfire, because it takes you out of the moment and reduces your engagement—which is precisely the thing that would lead to results in the first place. It's like rushing through a good meal just to get it done, or reading a quick summary of a classic novel so you can cut to the chase and see how it ends!

Try this: Play around with activities with no other goal in mind but to enjoy them for what they are, in the moment. Even 5 to 10 minutes of deep engagement can reset your mood and have you feeling more stable, balanced, and self-composed.

Be Ruthless With Distractions

People who understand how to be calm, collected, and self-controlled are people who know the importance of gathering and stilling their own minds.

Imagine that your conscious attention and awareness is like a beam of light. When that light is pulled together and collected into a strong, single beam, you can shine it on the things in your world—physical sensations, ideas, thoughts, emotions—and see these things with more clarity.

Focused, gathered attention is like a flashlight in the dark. In a very real way, your attentive awareness helps you navigate the world and lets you *see where you're going*.

But what happens when that beam of light is weak, scattered, or diffused? It's like a flashlight beam that's too wide—because it shines everywhere, it shines nowhere. It's too diluted to reveal much with any clarity.

Distractions and interruptions scatter the light of your focused, attentive awareness. Not only do they destroy flow and engagement, but they also make life pretty hard to navigate!

Unbothered people are *undistractable* people.

Their sense of purpose, intention, action, and awareness all shine in *one direction*, and they are simply not interested in whatever's on the periphery. In an almost literal sense, they don't *see* things that are irrelevant to their purposes.

They only see the object of their attention.

This kind of focus is both the cause and the effect of engaged flow:

- The more engaged and in flow you are, the less likely it is that you'll be distracted and interrupted.
- The harder you work at avoiding distractions and interruptions, the easier you will find it to achieve an engaged flow state.

In other words, focus → flow → focus.

To get this self-reinforcing "virtuous cycle" going, though, you have to begin with a little self-disciplined concentration. Here are some ideas.

- **Cut digital noise.** We'll explore this vital concept more in a later chapter. Kill any unnecessary notifications, install social media blockers and productivity apps, put devices on silent or in another room, or simply find ways to work offline and away from screens entirely.

- **Remove clutter.** Material clutter in your workspace reflects mental clutter... and makes that mental clutter worse. Remove everything from your work area that's not related to the task at hand. Remove any irrelevant stimuli; it should be impossible to engage with anything *but* your chosen task.
- **Find a rhythm between work and rest.** Schedule your most challenging tasks for the time of day you feel most alert and energized. Find a good sprint-then-rest pace, so you are alternating intense focus with shorts periods of constructive recovery. You might find, for example, that you work best when you give yourself tiny minute-long breaks throughout the hour where you pause, gather yourself and dive back in. Flow is never over-exertion. Why? Because if you're fatigued, you're more distractable.

If you're currently suffering from a fractured attention span, a screen addiction, or a tendency to self-distract whenever a task gets challenging, don't worry—it *will* take a little while to slowly ramp up your attentional stamina.

However, remember the **focus → flow → focus cycle** and know that discipline today will feel like effortlessness, ease, and flow tomorrow. It's hard, but it's worth it.

Strengthen Your Resilience With PERMA: Reach Out and Connect

The **R** in **PERMA** is for **R**elationships—healthy and happy ones, that is!

People need people, and it's no surprise that Seligman includes human connection as one of his five "good life" pillars.

Here, relationships mean *any* connection with another human being:

- Romantic connections, partners, spouses
- Family members
- Friends of all stripes
- Colleagues, bosses, mentors, employees
- Acquaintances, neighbors, and community members

A healthy and thriving social network is like an external immune system. When you feel seen, heard, supported, loved, and valued for who you are, *you feel stronger*. Better able to cope with life. Unbotherable.

Humans are relational creatures and cannot be healthy when isolated or disconnected—and that's a scientific fact. Good relationships:

- Keep you sharp and prevent cognitive decline in later years (Siedlecki et al., 2014).
- Help you live longer (Holt-Lunstad et al., 2015).

- Reduce your risk of depression and anxiety, and increase your emotional resilience (Liu et al., 2022).
- Give you better inflammatory and cardiovascular health (Yang et al., 2016).
- Help you recover from major health events like heart attacks (Berkman et al., 1992).
- Increase your self-esteem (Orth, Robins & Meier, 2021).
- Are associated with better immune (Kawachi et al., 2005) and neuroendocrine function (Uchino, 2006).

It's obvious: **If you want to increase resilience, then strengthen your social network.**

How?

Try this: Make an effort. That's all.

Forging and maintaining relationships takes time, but you don't need a lifelong soulmate or a dozen best friends to start deriving benefits from being more socially connected.

- **Just reach out.** Ask questions, show interest, and keep in touch. Pay attention to the people around you and show genuine concern for them. Be a better listener. Is there someone you haven't connected with in a while? Send them a message or give them a call.
- **Draw on "weak links."** Every person you know knows someone else you might really

get on with. Say yes to invitations, even those you're not 100% sure about, and try to cultivate these "weak links" —i.e., the people on the very periphery of your social network.
- **Get out there.** Even if you don't connect super deeply with people, there is value in being in one another's company, in conversation, and in doing activities together. Join a group or class, volunteer, work in your community, or join a choir or sports group. You don't have to be instant best friends with people to enjoy a sense of belonging and community.

Build Life Satisfaction With PERMA: Set Goals and Achieve Them

If you can cultivate positive emotions and create more gratitude in your life, if you can increase flow and engagement in everything you do, or if you can improve the quality of your relationships, then, according to Seligman, you are on your way to generating a life that is rich and fulfilling.

If even one of these areas is reinforced, your ability to stay calm, unbothered, and mentally tough will dramatically improve. **Practicing *all five together* creates a balanced, sustainable form of resilience that really will feel solid and unshakable, no matter what life throws at you.**

In this chapter, let's look at the final two letters in the PERMA acronym:

M for **M**eaning.

A for **A**ccomplishments (sometimes "**A**chievements")

There's a reason these two will be considered together.

Human beings have a need for meaning that's just as strong as our need for food, sleep, or air.

- We want to feel that our worlds are intelligible and make sense.
- We want to know that we have a place in that world, and that we belong somewhere.
- We need to have a feeling of our worth as human beings, and that our contributions are valuable.
- We need to know who we are, what we're here for, and what our purpose is.

Now, if you look closely, you will see that all of these questions of meaning are closely tied to questions of accomplishment, achievement, and attainment.

There is no achievement without meaning, and no meaning without achievement.

In order to belong, to contribute, to make sense to ourselves and others, and to feel like we have value, our behavior needs to have *a direction.* It needs to be *for* something, and *towards* something—in other words, our lives need to be in the service of some goal, however loosely defined.

What, then, is a human being's purpose in life?

Well, thankfully, this isn't a book about the meaning of life. But it *is* about the importance of having some understanding within yourself about how you'll answer life's Big Questions.

What matters?

- Mastering a profession or devoting yourself to a calling?
- Fame, success, wealth, and status?
- Creative pursuits, beauty, self-expression, art?
- Love, family, human connection, and service?
- Spiritual truth?
- The acquisition of knowledge, wisdom, and experience?
- Having a good time?

There is of course no consensus on what exact activities make a meaningful life, but one thing is true: Those people who claim to have a life purpose tend to live longer, and have happier and more fulfilling lives (Kashdan et al., 2009).

Fortunately or unfortunately, **there really is no substitute when it comes to meaning, no cheat codes, and no shortcuts**. That means that we cannot simply adopt the values of those around us or assume that if something gives someone else a sense of purpose, then it will do the same for us.

Not sure what ultimately matters to you? That's OK! Figuring it out is part of the fun, and the more time and energy you invest in the process, the more satisfying you'll find the outcome.

Try this:

- **Don't make assumptions, but experiment.** People can be pretty bad at predicting what will actually make them happy in life. We may just assume that ease, wealth, and pleasure are what we want, when in reality, these things might not scratch those deeper existential itches.
- **Try out something new.** Volunteer, get involved in a cause, take up a new hobby, or spend time with a person you might have ordinarily overlooked. Do hard things. Challenge yourself to try something different.
- **Look honestly at your life so far.** Your feelings about your life path so far hold valuable insights about what matters in the long run.
- **What are you especially proud of?** Look closely at the things that currently provide a sense of fulfilment, satisfaction, and identity, and see what that says about your values and principles.

- **What are you ashamed or regretful about?** The actions that you least want to associate yourself with can hint at occasions where you may have violated your own principles.
- **What has never changed?** People change all throughout their lives, of course. But can you identify a single thread that runs through your entire life so far? Something that makes you who you are, on a soul level? The things that stay stable despite changes in circumstances are often the things most connected to your deeper sense of meaning and purpose.
- **Think about the people around you.** Sometimes, we understand ourselves best by understanding ourselves in relation to others.
- **Who do you most admire?** And what does that admiration tell you about your values?
- **Who do you judge most, condemn, or hope never to be like?** Think about what the *opposite* traits and characteristics may be.
- **Who is closest to you?** Think carefully about what your deepest and most cherished relationships might tell you about yourself. The thing you feel that this person provides you? It's often closely connected to the thing you are most earnestly seeking in life.

OK, let's zoom out from the heavy stuff for a second.

We don't have to figure everything out all at once, and too much navel-gazing can be counterproductive.

In fact, one of the best ways to identify those activities that will imbue your life with the most meaning is to actually *do them*... and then observe how much satisfaction and fulfilment you feel afterwards.

This is the **A** in **PERMA** – **A**ccomplishments and **A**chievements. We can also say that the A stands for **A**ction—the willingness to make meaning *real* in the world.

Real life satisfaction goes well beyond gold stars, promotions, or social media likes. **Real achievement is deep, engaged flow with an activity that is intrinsically meaningful to you.**

- Without flow, engagement, or meaning, achievement will always feel hollow.
- Without action, values and principles are just as empty.

Seligman explains that accomplishment is essential for a sense of self-worth, direction, and satisfaction. Accomplishment means:

- Completion and finishing what you start
- A feeling of pride and self-esteem

- The sense that you are developing and improving
- A feeling of mastery and competence—the knowledge that *you can do it*
- The acquisition of discipline, patience, and perseverance—the knowledge that you can do it *even if it's hard*

Unbothered, self-regulated people derive much of their resilience and self-worth from the strength and continuity of their own actions over time. They set goals and achieve them. They trust in themselves.

It's not about the kind of goal, or the size, but the conscious decision to *act towards something*, then get there using your own will and intention.

Engaging with life this way is about so much more than reaching the finish line or winning a trophy. Attaining intrinsically motivated goals always brings greater rewards than it first seems… including a taste for growth and evolution *for its own sake.*

Three Practical Ways to Have a More Satisfying Life

End Your Day With a Win Log

Try this: At the end of every day, take a moment to write down something that you've achieved, no matter how small and insignificant it may seem.

In the same way as we can carelessly skip over our blessings, we can also fail to recognize and celebrate all the good things we've actually accomplished. Instead of hurrying onto the next task or challenge, give yourself an opportunity to acknowledge your gains.

- I was tired and feeling lazy, but I still read 10 pages of my book like I said I would *(that proves that I am a disciplined person)*.
- I managed not to lose my patience during that difficult meeting today *(that shows that day by day, my emotional regulation is improving)*.
- I put together a really healthy and delicious dinner for myself *(that means that I can trust myself to make healthy decisions)*.

Don't let these small wins be invisible. The more confident you can feel in the everyday progress you're making, the more unshakeable you'll be in the face of everyday setbacks.

You'll notice that *what matters is how you connect your achievement to some bigger meaning.*

There's no point reading 10 pages of a book if you don't care about reading and the book is irrelevant to you. However, if you value focused self-discipline, and you care about what's in that book, reading it will give you a fantastic sense of satisfaction.

Don't Be Afraid to Challenge Yourself

Playing small can feel like a smart move sometimes, but over time, under-challenging yourself can lead to apathy and boredom.

Growth happens outside of your comfort zone, and that means that if you want the satisfaction of achievement, you'll often have to embrace a degree of discomfort first.

If you **learn to see this discomfort as a sign that you're on the right path**, however, then you won't be discouraged or demotivated.

Try this: Make a habit of setting goals that are ever so slightly too large for you. You likely already know that goals should be SMART, i.e.,

- Specific
- Measurable
- Achievable
- Realistic
- and Time bound

But don't make them too *easy*.

Set a goal that is 5% more challenging or audacious than you're comfortable setting. This will sharpen your focus, push you to work hard… and turbo-charge your sense of satisfaction when you accomplish it!

Reframe Failure

Want to be unflappable in life?

Then set your own terms.

If you are intrinsically motivated, then YOU are the one who decides what things mean, and why.

Did you know that you are at liberty to interpret "failure" in any way you like?

Many people fail to set goals and work hard towards them because, simply, they're afraid of failure.

Try this: Decide within yourself that as long as you learn something from the process, then there is no such thing as failure. Every outcome is useful for a person willing to learn from the experience.

- *It didn't work?* You've learned something valuable about how not to do it.
- *It's taking longer than you thought?* You've learned something valuable about patience, practice, and perseverance.
- *It's not what you wanted after all?* You've learned something valuable about how never to make that mistake again.

Remember that **Achievement and Meaning are connected**. No matter the outcome, *you* can choose how you make sense of it, how you interpret it, and what it means to you.

Meaning and Resilience

Before we end this section, it's worth exploring one more powerful way that a healthy sense of meaning and purposes can inoculate us against life's challenges. Not only can we derive meaning from achieving our life's goals and purposes, but we also build resilience in the face of adversity.

Nietzsche reminds us that, "He who has a **why** to live can bear almost any **how**." In other words, if you have a strong sense of your own purpose in life, you are resilient.

You're able to endure adversity, suffering, and challenge.

You can dig deep and find true strength.

Sometimes, you discover that you can do more than you even believed possible.

We all need a reason to get out of bed in the morning, but we need more than that: We need a reason to keep pushing, to get back up again after a setback, and to bear with life's everyday annoyances, injustices, and disappointments.

The big idea: Mental fortitude is not about you. It's about what you're *for*. It's about what you believe in, what you stand for, and who you're trying to become.

Any person can have natural personal strength or can rely on their innate powers to a certain point. But a person cannot go *beyond* this strength unless their lives are connected to something bigger than themselves.

The bigger and more rock-solid your WHY, the smaller your everyday troubles will seem in comparison.

The more permanent your ultimate purpose, the less anything can shake or move you.

Let's look at what this means in everyday life.

Step 1: Identify What Matters

Remember that the most powerful *whys* are those that are big—bigger than you and your human ego.

While you can find long lists out there, core values are seldom captured in single abstract words like "kindness" or "innovation." Core values are more like systems of belief or sets of guiding principles that act as a structure and framework for nothing less than reality itself, and your place in it.

Your core values speak to the ideology and philosophy that organize and make sense of your world.

Your core values are the compass that guides you, and that means that they act like standards against which your own behavior can be measured. **Your values are the center—and your behavior flows out from that center.**

This means that at any one point in time, you are either living according to those values and principles, or you're not; either you're "on purpose" or you're not.

Step 2: Connect Every Action to Purpose

The next step follows naturally from the first. Once you've identified your values, then you automatically know what actions to take: anything that brings you closer to that purpose!

Your behavior is no longer determined by chance, the whims of other people, struggle or adversity, or random temptations and distractions. It is, and always is, determined by your values.

Your values always point in the same direction, like a compass.

And you follow, not bothered, not confused.

And it's *that* consistency and devotion that makes you strong, unflappable, and ultra-resilient.

Summary:

- Positive psychology focuses on solutions and strengths, not just disease, disorder, or impaired function. Seligman's 5 factor PERMA model lists the building blocks of a flourishing life: Positive emotions, Engagement, Relationships, Meaning, and Accomplishment.
- Gratitude is a way to proactively build positive emotion and keep your focus on all

the blessings that are already in your life. Bring continued, hopeful, and expectant attention to your world.
- Focus on genuine feelings of thankfulness, and be sure to stamp out complaining. Remember that complaining is passive ingratitude. Instead, build gratitude rituals into your everyday routine.
- Deep engagement is a remedy for anxiety, mindlessness, boredom, and overwhelm. Flow creates more richness, depth, and reward. To engage, simply be present—even with mundane tasks. Purposefully schedule one flow activity a day—without distractions and without focusing on the outcome. Be focused: focus → flow → focus.
- Humans are relational beings; if you want to increase psychological resilience, bolster your social network.
- Increase feelings of life satisfaction and meaning by setting goals and achieving them. Our behavior needs to have a direction to be meaningful. Seek intrinsically motivated goals. Challenge yourself, celebrate wins, and reframe failures. The bigger and more rock-solid your WHY, the smaller your everyday troubles will seem in comparison.

Section 3: The Wisdom of the Stoics

"God, grant me the serenity to accept the things I cannot change, the courage to change the things I can, and the wisdom to know the difference."

- Reinhold Niebuhr

Control What You Can, Let Go of What You Can't

The famous "Serenity Prayer" above is popular for a very good reason: It works.

While recognizable today as an old Christian favorite, the spirit of the Serenity Prayer actually has an older pedigree, which speaks to the wisdom of the ancient Greek Stoic philosophers. Going back even further still, the philosophy expounded in the *Tao te Ching* also explores this fundamental dynamism between stillness and motion, yielding and force, yin and yang.

The big idea is pretty simple: **Peace is about balance**.

To be truly calm within ourselves, we need to have a crystal-clear understanding of what is in our control, and what isn't.

- Sometimes we need to act.
- Sometimes we need to accept that we *cannot* act.

True wisdom does not lie in finding out how to bend everything to our will, nor does it lie in passively accepting whatever comes our way. Rather, it's about *timing*—when to advance, and when to retreat. When to push, and when to let go. When to work, and when to recover.

One of your strongest shields against stress is clarity about what's under your control.

Life is certainly exhausting and confusing sometimes, but we make it more so when we try to control things that we cannot—for example, other people's thoughts, feelings, and actions.

People who are unbothered are people who quite literally do not allow themselves to be disturbed by those things over which they have no control.

Wisdom means discerning the difference. And foolishness? There are *two* types:

1. **Trying to control things you don't have control over** = depletion, frustration, stress, anxiety, and anger.

2. **Failing to control what *is* under your control** = disappointment, regret, impotence, apathy, missed opportunity, and waste.

Three Practical Ways to Find Balance and Wisdom

In popular culture, the Stoicism is often portrayed as "mastering your emotions." But the truth is that wisdom is more about learning to accurately identify and classify the circumstances that unfold around you—which means there will be less emotional reactivity to master.

Important: There is nothing intrinsically wrong with strong emotion, nor is the Stoic's goal to be numb, invulnerable, or emotionally shut down.

Wisdom is not like a brick wall or a weapon of war. It's more like a *finely calibrated filter* that allows you to perceive clearly, so that you can hold onto what is of value and let worthless things pass by without unsettling you.

Ask the Control Question

When you *do* feel unsettled, get into the habit of pausing and asking yourself,

"Is this within my control?"

If not, then let it go.

Some things that are 100% not in your control:

- A person at work dislikes you for no reason.
- You planned a picnic but now it's raining.
- You were born short, not tall.
- You caught a cold and now you feel rotten.
- You missed winning the lottery by one number.

We can all logically see that these things are not in our control, but sometimes, **strong emotions can cloud our judgment**. We make an error: because we *feel* strongly about a situation, we assume we are somehow involved with it, somehow invested in its unfolding.

For example: You may feel stressed out about the outcome of an election. Really, really, *really* stressed out. You have opinions. You have thoughts and feelings. Strong ones.

But so what?

Is it in your power to control the way that millions of people vote? Of course not. Your zone of control includes only *your* vote. And that's true no matter how strongly you feel about the situation.

Strong feelings are understandable and only human. But it's worth remembering that these emotions are ultimately useless, and a waste of your energy. Why? Because after you're done having them, you will be in precisely the same position you are in now.

Why not just be in the position you are in now but *without* the additional stress?

Try a Three-Column List

Now, not everything in life is this black and white.

If your genes determine that you are short, your adult height is more or less fixed, and there is nothing you can do about it.

However, what if your genes determine that you are at a slightly higher risk of developing type 2 diabetes? Your genes might give you a predisposition to developing type 2 diabetes, but your actions and choices play a big role, too. After all, you could choose to live a healthy life and never get diabetes.

Long story short: **When it comes to what is under our control and what isn't, most things in life are not 100% one or the other.**

Try this: Divide an A4 sheet of paper into three columns, with these headings:

1. In my control
2. Partly in my control
3. Not in my control

Now, whatever's bothering you, give yourself some time to slowly untangle it, thread by thread. Sometimes a big problem, when analyzed, is actually quite simple. On the other hand, a small problem can reveal itself to be a cluster of many smaller, separate problems.

With calm, neutral eyes, look at each thought and idea and categorize it into one of the three columns above. The act of carefully sorting ideas and assumptions alone is an illuminating exercise.

Example: You have failed an important exam or test, and you're devastated.

Step 1: You draw your three columns and pick your way through the knot of thoughts and feelings in your head.

- You failed → Unless you invent a time machine, not in your control.
- You can re-sit the exam, but only in 6 months' time → Not in your control.
- You can choose to actually sign up for that next exam → In your control.
- You're devastated → Partly or all in your control.
- You can try again and study harder → In your control.
- You're delayed in earning your bigger qualification → Not in your control.
- You're angry and ashamed about being delayed → In your control.
- You find the subject matter really difficult → Partly in your control.
- Etc.

While this exercise may seem tedious, it's worth finely discerning the difference between the unchangeable fact that you failed, for example, and your quite changeable *response* to that fact.

Step 2: Everything that you have listed in the "not in my control" column? Get rid of it. Forget about it. You might like to even tear that column off the rest of the paper and burn it or throw it away. Let it go. It doesn't matter.

Step 3: Now look at everything that is 100% in your control. Convert everything in this column into an action step:

- Book to re-sit the exam.
- Decide in yourself that you will no longer entertain feelings of anger and shame.
- Make a new and improved study plan for next time. Hire a tutor, sign up for extra lessons, buy a book—you get the idea.

Step 4: Then move onto those things you have partial control over. Ask, **"Where do I need to practice acceptance, and where do I need to act?"**

You find the subject difficult? Well, every person has cognitive limits. Still, we can all work hard to achieve within our given range of potential. We can practice accepting our struggle, while simultaneously committing to act where we can. That may mean seeking out extra help and support.

Acceptance vs. action—find the balance.

Practice Daily Release

Have you ever tried to walk a long way on very soft, deep beach sand?

There's a lot of friction, so you get tired pretty quickly.

Life is the same: **The more friction, the more quickly you'll get tired**. In this analogy, *friction* is really the total of every tiny bit of resistance, frustration, and annoyance that daily life foists on us.

Pushing up against a big immovable object will wear you out pretty quickly, but pushing against hundreds of tiny little immovable objects will wear you out all the same over time.

Try this: Adopt the practice of actively letting go of these tiny, accumulated tensions, *every single day.* Think of it as a kind of daily mental hygiene.

Before bed, do a quick scan over your body and mind, and look for:

- Any signs of weariness
- Any psychological knots
- Any mental snags

Then *symbolically let them go.*

You may find you need to literally relax your muscles to let it go, or it may work to just visualize tensions dissolving or floating away.

One alternative is to say out loud: "I'm not carrying this anymore. Goodbye," and then focus on the feeling of relief, and that sweet return of your own serenity.

Another option is to write things in a "worry journal" and, when your mind wants to return to that thought, remind yourself that you don't have to think about it anymore, because it's in the journal.

Close the cover of the journal and draw a line in the sand.

Practice Negative Visualization

Today, *positive* visualization is in fashion. People are told to imagine what they want—imagine it vividly—and trust that their positivity and expectation alone will manifest their heart's desire.

We're told that healthy, successful people keep their chins up and *think positively*. The self-help gurus suggest affirmations, gutsy ambition, and techniques for carefully rewiring your thinking so that you know, deep down, that you can achieve your dreams, if only you believe in yourself.

But all this positivity has a dark side, and you may already be familiar with it: toxic positivity. This is forced optimism and an unwillingness and inability to engage with "negative" emotions.

Toxic positivity...

- **Can encourage us to invalidate and suppress our genuine emotions**, which actually only worsens depression and anxiety over time.
- **Can teach us to be ashamed of perfectly normal emotional reactions**, setting up unhealthy expectations of what life should feel like.
- **Can reduce our emotional awareness**, dampen our emotional literacy, and ultimately prevent us from learning to *manage* our emotions.
- **Can make us ungrateful and demanding**, since we not only come to hope for and expect good things, but we feel *entitled* to them... making our ordinary lives look insufficient compared to our expectations.
- **Can make us fragile and eternally disappointed.** After all, if we have a demand on reality that it always feels good and positive, how will we respond when it isn't?

Occasionally, the Stoic philosophers are imagined to be strong, unemotional, and invulnerable. It may come as a surprise, then, to learn that the Stoics actually promoted a personal development technique that encourages *negative* visualization, i.e., actively dwelling on the possibility of a bad outcome. Think of it as the ultimate antidote to toxic positivity.

Let's clarify here.

Negative visualization, or *premeditatio melorum*, is about consciously choosing to contemplate the worst-case scenario.

It is *not* the same as anxious rumination, pessimism, or catastrophizing.

Here's how it's different:

- **It builds gratitude**, encouraging you to appreciate what you actually have right now.
- **It builds resilience**, since it allows you to desensitize yourself to unwanted outcomes, which takes away the power they have over you.
- **It's logical**, since it helps you create a practical, realistic plan to prepare and cope with possible adversity, rather than just blindly fearing it.
- **It resets your perspective** and reminds you of the fleeting nature of life. This inspires you to make the very best of it right now, while you still can.

Three Practical Ways to Use the Power of Negativity

Negative Visualization, the Paradoxical Technique

A relentless focus on the positive actually increases the power of negativity over our lives, but negative visualization does the opposite: By *facing the negative* we gain mastery and control over it. And that's a pretty positive thing.

Here's how it works.

- **Step 1: Think about the things you value and care about.**
- This could be a loved one, a job, a possession, an everyday pleasure or luxury, your health, your home, or your general life circumstances.
- For extra effectiveness, choose those things you're likely to take for granted, or even the things you're currently a little dissatisfied with.
- **Step 2: Imagine losing these things.**
- Picture a future where you simply no longer have this thing you value.
- You can imagine a tragedy or setback, or simply picture what it would be like for this thing to never have existed in the first place.
- **Step 3: Be grateful. Find renewed contentment.**
- If you're doing step 1 and 2 right, step 3 should be almost automatic.
- Really imagine how it would feel to lose this thing, and then focus on that relieved sense of gratitude that—hooray!—you actually get to keep the thing you care about. What a powerful perspective check.
- **Step 4: Prepare and be practical.**
- You're not just thinking of the misery of a negative outcome, but facing it square on and

giving yourself the opportunity to think through it pragmatically.
- How would you cope? What would happen next? Would it be as bad as you predict?

For those of us raised on a steady diet of "good vibes only," such an exercise can feel tricky, even a little dangerous. But it's essential that you see the difference between mere *dwelling* on negativity, and ***facing it*, constructively.**

When you ruminate, complain, take things for granted, or catastrophize over worst-case scenarios, you're actually not preparing for that negative outcome, nor are you desensitizing yourself. All you're doing, psychologically speaking, is picking at a scab.

To illustrate this point, imagine a man who is utterly terrified of losing his job, and so he wastes countless stressful hours overthinking. He keeps thinking, "If I lose my job, it's all over. My life will be ruined. I won't survive. It'll be the worst thing that'll ever happen to me. I don't know what I'd do…"

On and on he goes.

Resilient, self-controlled, unbothered people **don't fear** a bad outcome.

They **anticipate** it.

They *know* life can be hard. And they face the scary bits head on, so that when/if something happens, they're not surprised. They're not afraid. They're not angry or offended or confused.

They're not bothered.

Why? Because they've already mentally rehearsed many times over how they'll cope.

This is like a man noticing that his job may be insecure, visualizing in detail how he might lose it… and *then* imagining how he might pick up the pieces, find another job, and move on. He allows his fear to inspire a plan. His mind feels out the contours of a possible future that a more anxious person might be too afraid to explore.

His active planning does a few things:

- It helps him be relieved and grateful for the fact that he actually does have a job right now.
- It helps him take practical steps to prepare for the possibility that he does lose his job.
- It takes the power and sting away from the fear he has. Instead of ruminating endlessly, "I don't know what I'd do…" he can stare it squarely in the eyes. "So what would I do? Let me think about it, step by step."

The antidote to catastrophizing, ruminating, and negative thinking is not positive thinking. It's engaging with your negative thoughts in a strategic and productive way.

Adjust Expectations With a Morning Ritual

In Marcus Aurelius' *Meditations*, we find the following sage advice:

> *When you wake up in the morning, tell yourself: The people I deal with today will be meddling, ungrateful, arrogant, dishonest, jealous, and surly. They are like this because they can't tell good from evil. But I have seen the beauty of good, and the ugliness of evil, and have recognized that the wrongdoer has a nature related to my own—not of the same blood or birth, but the same mind, and possessing a share of the divine. And so none of them can hurt me. No one can implicate me in ugliness. Nor can I feel angry at my relative, or hate him. We were born to work together like feet, hands, and eyes, like the two rows of teeth, upper and lower. To obstruct each other is unnatural. To feel anger at someone, to turn your back on him: These are obstructions.*

This is not the conventional advice, right?

Aurelius is telling us *not* to wake up in the morning thinking,

"Today, I receive abundance in unexpected ways."

"I attract what is meant for me."

"I create my reality."

If you genuinely believe the above, you're in for a world of resentment, confusion, and disappointment when you encounter people who are "meddling, ungrateful, arrogant, dishonest, jealous, and surly."

You do not create your reality. You live in reality and are free to create your response to it.

In a way, Aurelius' advice is more positive and more compassionate than the conventional advice precisely because of its realism. He tells us that people suck and will continue to suck—but as inevitable and annoying as that is, we can and should continue to work with them, because they're like us, and we're like them.

Keep your eye on the "share of the divine" you both possess—and don't be bothered by the rest.

Use Negative Visualization to Reset With Gratitude

Premeditatio melorum does not have to be a purely abstract, intellectual exercise. While you can use the technique in a hypothetical way, it's often more powerful when **applied** as and when you need it in everyday life.

For example:

- **In relationships.** Feeling irritated by their little foibles and annoying habits? Instead of focusing on their faults and failures, imagine

your life without this person in it at all. Imagine that this petty argument is the last time you ever talk. This will reset your perspective: This person can certainly be infuriating, but aren't they *on the whole* a blessing to you?
- **At work.** Feeling bogged down, bored, or resentful about the work you have to do? Instead of comparing your situation to some perfect ideal, instead imagine you're unemployed and struggling to find work. Imagine the stress. The financial insecurity. The low self-esteem. Your job might still be wrong for you, but your attitude towards it will be tempered somewhat.
- **Concerning your health or appearance.** Unhappy about how you look? Your weight or age? Feel irritated with little health complaints? Meditate on the fact that soon, you'll be dead and in the ground, *without any life in you at all.* Your body may not be perfect now, but today, you have life. You have time. In fact, knowing that you have health today but that it's not guaranteed for tomorrow, what proactive steps can you take right now to protect and extend the vitality you *do* have?
- **In everyday life.** Feeling bored and uninspired? Lazy? Take a cold shower. Those icy needles of water hitting your bare skin are the perfect counterargument for taking your everyday luxuries and comforts for

granted! Plus, the rush of warmth and energy you feel *afterwards* will recalibrate your reward system and remind you that mindless habits, instant gratification, and cheap ease will never truly fulfil you.

Respond With Indifference: Starve Negativity of Power

Most people don't understand what *indifference* really means.

It's not about being cold, aloof, haughty, unfeeling, rude, mean, careless, dismissive, bored, or weary.

Very simply, being indifferent just means that a certain stimulus *makes no difference* to you. Importantly, that means that you don't resist it, nor do you cling to it. You don't love it, but you also don't hate it. You're not afraid of it, but neither are you spending any energy being actively brave.

You are truly neutral.

You are simply not responding.

You have not granted it any of your interest, awareness, or attention.

Indifference is not +1 and it's not -1... it's 0.

Forcefully trying to convince yourself you're not bothered? That's being bothered, just in the opposite direction!

Sadly, people can suffer from a kind of "pendulum effect."

They begin with a tendency to:

- Have weak boundaries
- Get too caught up with things
- Over-identify and fuse with events and emotions
- Overreact

But then they *overcorrect* that tendency and go to the other extreme by:

- Making their boundaries too rigid
- Acting with rudeness, coldness, or disregard that borders on hostility
- Disconnecting from everything and everyone
- Under-reacting

The irony is that both ends of the pendulum are just mirrors of one another; both are forms of reactivity.

Our goal: finding that still, balanced point in the middle.

The Stoics taught NONREACTIVITY in the face of provocation, insult, injury, or adversity.

This doesn't mean that your goal should be to have no emotions, only that your emotions are under your conscious control, not the other way around.

We want to be *emotionally regulated*, not *emotionally neutered*! That means that we take responsibility for managing and directing our own emotional experience, rather than letting random external events push us this way and that.

Mental toughness is not about never feeling things; it's about cultivating composure and stillness in a world that is constantly tempting you to feel everything.

In the Stoics' day, insult and provocation was largely a to-your-face affair. If you encountered nasty gossip, criticism, or attacks, it would usually be in person. Today? Our social landscape could not be more different, and most of us face negativity in a form that the Stoics could scarcely have imagined: the internet.

Today, dark algorithms, AI, and hostile financial interests mean that **the internet is basically a negativity engine.**

- The news media offers an infinite supply of emotionally triggering headlines that elicit hate, fear, exhaustion, despair, and confusion.
- Social media exacerbates feelings of inferiority, jealousy, shame, and judgment.
- Pornography kindles, intensifies, and distorts sexual desire.
- "Angertainment" amplifies feelings of outrage.

- Gaming, forums, and other platforms can generate apathy, restlessness, and self-absorption.
- Online shopping platforms, marketing, and ads fuel dissatisfaction, greed, and the never-ending desire for *more.*

Are you one of those people who only uses the internet for wholesome, useful purposes? Congratulations. Also, the following advice doesn't apply to you.

However, if you're like the rest of us, the internet has a hold on your mind, body, and soul... and the power it has over you rests purely in its ability to activate your emotions.

Even though the Stoics didn't have to deal with the emotional fallout of Instagram or TikTok, they knew thousands of years ago that **the only way to be truly free is to be immune to emotional manipulation.**

In other words, **indifference is a powerful shield against everything in the world that deliberately seeks to control, disturb, disrupt, or influence you via your emotions.**

When you can respond to a stimulus with calm indifference, that stimulus loses its power over you.

It cannot move you.

It cannot decide on your behalf how you will feel, or how you will act.

Only *you* get to decide that.

That's the magic of emotional indifference.

The Stoics taught that if a stranger randomly insults you to your face, the wisest course of action is to be silent, composed, and self-controlled. Walk away. Refuse to be ruffled.

Sounds good, right?

Yet…

- How many of us are easily frothed up into a rage when we read a hateful comment online?
- How often do we get stirred up into fear and panic because of some distressing news story?
- How often do we descend into self-criticism and self-loathing because of some glossy celebrity or influencer we've seen online?

We need to learn to be like the ancient Stoics, and cultivate the modern version of self-control, dignified composure, and the **quiet refusal to be ruffled against our will.**

Three Practical Ways to Be Less Emotionally Reactive

The bad news is that the world—especially the online world—will continue to provoke and trigger us so long as it's profitable to do so.

The good news is that these triggers and influences only have as much control over us as we are willing to grant them.

Read that again: *Unless you respond emotionally*, these influences are utterly impotent and can do nothing to you.

Have No Opinion

Here is a modern invention: the idea that everybody is "entitled to their opinion."

Have you considered that you don't always need to form an opinion? Is it possible that it is not always necessary—or even desirable—to form a personal view on this or that?

The thing is, **when you form an opinion, you also form an emotional attachment**. You invest yourself. You stake a claim, and now you have skin in the game. And *that* means that you are now available to be emotionally disturbed or upset.

Don't misunderstand: A person cannot live without preferences, values, and principles. However, we don't need to form an opinion about *everything*.

Recall that wisdom means knowing the difference between what is and isn't under our control. Let's expand this to say that **wisdom also includes knowing what is and isn't for us to evaluate.**

Sometimes, a stimulus will arise in our field of awareness. But as we've already seen, that doesn't mean we are *compelled* to react to it. That stimulus exists, but that doesn't automatically grant it the right to our attention or emotional energy.

We can take a little too much enjoyment in being offended. We all relish righteous indignation from time to time, right? But beware—it's a trap!

Remember the words of Brigham Young: *"He who takes offense when no offense is intended is a fool, and he who takes offense when offense is intended is a greater fool."*

- **Seen something controversial or emotive in the news?** Instead of jumping to decide whose side you're on or what you think about it, just try… not doing that. Notice how life unfolds as it will, whether you're emotionally hooked into it or not. Notice how it feels to just say, "I have no opinion about that."
- **Is there a disagreement or conflict unfolding around you?** Who says you have to take part? Practice real neutrality. Things are stirred up, then they pass again. Another

thing arises to take its place. So what? Feel the freedom that comes with choosing *not* to go along with every new trend or disturbance.
- **Are circumstances changing around you?** Delay judgment. A sudden turn of events may prompt a knee-jerk response out of you, but wait a little while before you make bold pronouncements about what things mean. Life can move in strange and unpredictable ways—wise people avoid rash decisions. Even if you *do* make a judgment call on something, don't rush. Be slow to make big claims.

Disengage and Walk Away

If someone deliberately pokes or provokes you, pause. Just stop. Watch as any fleeting desire to retaliate or lash out comes… and then goes again.

Just smile and walk away.

That's it. You don't need to say something clever, and you certainly don't need to *show* the other person just how little they've bothered you (after all, that desire just proves how much you are bothered, right?).

Your lack of response should not be seen as a punishment you dole out, or a way to "be the bigger person." That's just vanity.

True indifference is feeling as though *nothing has happened*.

Just imagine that there's a thin coating of Teflon on you, and their negativity just slides right off. There's no force or effort—there's just nothing for that negativity to stick to.

It can be very tempting to get stuck in a retributive mindset—i.e., the feeling that an injustice has occurred (no matter how minor) and you cannot possibly rest until you've retaliated somehow. But the fact is you *can* rest. You *can* let it go.

The moment you decide not to be bothered by something, there is simply no way for it to touch you anymore. That's power. Revenge? That's distraction.

Examples:

- A rude stranger mutters something offensive under their breath as you walk past → You smile and keep on walking. You leave that comment right where it is—it's *theirs*, not yours, so why pick it up and take it with you?
- During a heated discussion, someone says something hurtful to get a rise out of you → You don't acknowledge it. You end the discussion. Talk again later when you're both calm—what's the point of taking turns hurting one another?

- At work, someone says something you know is untrue, unkind, or outright offensive → You walk away. You don't make it your business to correct, persuade, convince, or punish them. You don't bother yourself with forgiving them. You just *don't think of them at all*. Other people are wrong sometimes. Let them be.

Channel Your Energy Elsewhere

A triggering stimulus is basically a message that says to you, "Hey! I want your life force. Give it to me now, because I want to put it to use for my own purposes."

The amazing thing is how often we say "OK."

- While you're wasting time doomscrolling and fighting with people in comments sections, you're not living the life you've said you want to live.
- While you're getting caught up in unnecessary arguments, dramas, and misunderstandings, you're not building, learning, or growing.
- While you're nursing your wounded pride or an offended ego, you're not out there pouring energy into things you actually care about.

The next time something unreasonable demands to have your attention, time, awareness or emotional energy—i.e. your life force—politely decline.

Instead of wasting time thinking how you will or won't respond, just divert your attention altogether and direct it towards something that actually matters.

Take a walk or go to the gym.

Clean something.

Read, write, or study.

Have a conversation with someone about something entirely unrelated.

Go out into nature.

Build, cook, or repair something.

Whatever you do, get out of your reactive emotions and firmly back into the world.

Summary:

- Stoic philosophy and the Serentiy Prayer express the wisdom that peace lies in balance and timing. To be unbothered we need to be able to discern what is and isn't in our control, and act accordingly.
- Ask, "Is this in my control?" or try the three-column technique. Convert every worry that you have control over into action; release the rest, finding balance between acceptance and action. Practice a daily tension release to let go of accumulated mental frictions.
- The Stoic technique of negative visualization is about consciously choosing to

contemplate the worst-case scenario to increase gratitude and resilience, while allowing for practical planning and preparation. By facing the negative, we gain mastery and control over it. It's paradoxical, but a powerful antidote to toxic positivity.
- Expect and prepare for life being difficult sometimes. Face your fears plainly, and don't let the faults of others disturb you. Use negative visualization to reset your expectations and shift your perspective.
- Respond with indifference in the face of provocation, insult, injury, or adversity—no clinging, no resistance. Be careful of emotional manipulation—particularly online. Practice having no opinion, disengaging from negativity, and consciously channeling your emotional energy to where you want it to go.

Section 4: Peace is Simplicity

"The ability to simplify means to eliminate the unnecessary so that the necessary may speak."

- Hans Hofmann

Practice Calming Micro-Activities

There is a depressing but inevitable law of stress: The more triggered you are, the easier it is for you to get triggered. The more stressed you feel, the worse you are at coping with even small additional amounts of stress.

The result is a **self-reinforcing cycle of constant stimulation and over-reactivity.**

We may feel like, in ordinary circumstances, we're fairly level-headed and unflappable. Trouble is, we're so seldomly in "ordinary circumstances"! Instead, life always seems to be rushing along at breakneck pace, and we always seem to be running after it somehow, playing catch up.

What's the way out?

To answer that, let's consider a brief analogy: a cluttered house.

Imagine that you're having trouble living in a dangerously cluttered house, and it's high time to make some changes. Do you:

1. Take a whole two weeks off to painstakingly tidy everything up, once and for all.
2. Pay someone else to declutter for you.
3. Decide you'll just go on holiday whenever you get sick of looking at it all.
4. Commit to getting rid of one small piece of clutter every day.

Each of these things, in their own way, counts as a solution to the problem. But one is a better solution than the others!

In this analogy, the house is our mental space, and the clutter is all the accumulated stress, worry, tension, and strain we incur through the process of daily living.

A stressed-out person is a person whose mind is clogged and cluttered—it's hard to live in there, and everything moves more slowly and with more effort than it should.

What's the way out?

One option is to take dramatic, once-and-for-all action. You know the kind of thing—a major fix-up project, an overnight transformation, and a big-ticket life makeover. Other options include handing over responsibility for the problem to someone else, or just outright ignoring things.

I probably don't need to tell you why these things are not the solutions they appear to be.

The only real solution for everyday, cumulative stress is everyday, cumulative stress-relief.

In other words, *little and often.*

Everyday stress is cumulative, just like dirt or clutter. If we hope to stay on top of it, our efforts need to be cumulative too; i.e., we need to develop a stress-management *habit*.

Some wait until things build and then blow up before taking major action, but this in itself is stressful—and doesn't address the ongoing *habit* of stress.

Some passively blame people or circumstances for their stress or wait for someone else to save them—a therapist, a partner, a friend—but again, this doesn't address the cumulative *habit* of stress.

Some know the stress is there and deal with it by running away periodically, maybe with distraction, escapism, substance use, or plain old-fashioned denial. But—you guessed it—this won't work long-term because the underlying *habit* of stress remains intact.

Three Practical Ways to Make Stress-Management an Everyday Habit

Breathing Reset

Tight, shallow, or tense breathing is a foolproof early warning sign that your anxiety is ramping up. Often, however, we don't even notice that our breathing has become constricted and uncomfortable—or that we're actually holding our breath!

We need to deliberately pause, check in with ourselves, and consciously let go of whatever we're holding onto.

Breathing tensions that are ignored and allowed to accumulate soon become muscle tensions... and muscle tensions soon become mental and emotional discomfort, distress, or pain.

A few deep, loose breaths the very moment you first notice rising tension can stop the spiral before it gets a chance to start.

You can get ahead of mounting tension by building in little "breath breaks" all throughout your day.

- **Use breath as punctuation.** Take five slow breaths before starting a new task, or any time you switch focus, move to a new room, or change where you're putting your attention. It's a simple habit that brings more light, ease, and space into your day.

- **Exhales are passive.** Many of us unconsciously force out an exhale—but remember that relaxation is the absence of effort. Try a few active, deep inhales but then just *let* your entire body go loose and simply *allow* the air to escape. No force.
- **Slow down.** Hurried breathing typically reflects hurried thinking or emotional overwhelm. Slow down what's going on in your heart and mind by slowing down your breath. For a minute or two, close your eyes and control your breath so that you:
- Inhale for *four* counts
- Pause for two counts
- Exhale for *six* counts
- Pause again for two.
    - ➔ Having a longer exhale than inhale will gently calm you down.

Nature Glance

Breathing mindfully is the ultimate calming micro-activity, but there are many more options. Nature, in particular, has an almost magical way of helping the body to release, relax, and come back to baseline.

But it's not magic—there's solid scientific evidence that simply being in or around nature soothes the human nervous system. Research studies have confirmed that gazing at "foliage colors" (i.e. shades of green) has profound effects on mood (Briki & Majed, 2019) and natural spaces can create feelings of calmness and comfort (Kexiu et. al., 2021).

- **Step outside.** Try your best to get outside each and every day, whenever possible. Walk, gaze at the sky, breathe deeply, and just absorb. Whenever you get a moment, look out the window—especially first thing in the morning, when the natural sunlight can work to regulate your melatonin levels.
- **Bring nature in**. Growing things can teach us a lot about calm yet vibrant presence. Nature never rushes. Bring a few (more) leafy friends into your home or workspace so you are never far away from your daily green fix.
- **Get a pet.** Not a decision to make lightly, of course, but adopting an animal companion might lower cortisol levels, reduce blood pressure, and boost your mood (NIH newsletter, 2018, *The Power of Pets*).

Mini-Journaling

Stress-management and self-care routines don't have to be dramatic to have dramatic results.

Mini-journaling is a way to bring a little bright spot of mindfulness and self-regulation to your everyday flow.

Try this: Simply take a moment now and again to write down a sentence or two about how you're feeling. If you like, you can put down thoughts and ideas and gently rework them.

- I'm tense right now, but I know it will pass.
- I feel hopeful today.
- Mood is around 6/10. Grumpy but I don't know why!
- Surprised by how much I enjoyed that.
- Tired and bored with this task. Looking forward to something more exciting soon...

Writing—even if only briefly—brings clarity and awareness. The more you pay attention to the little things, the better you'll get at catching little fluctuations, and then gently bringing yourself back to your center again.

Chronic rumination and overthinking? Everything bothering you? It may be nothing more than the build-up of stress.

Here's the key: You won't have to cope with major stress blowouts if you deal with tensions when they're still minor. **Master the art of continual, subtle course-correction**, and few things will seriously disturb you.

Scale Down Digital Noise

We've already explored the potentially toxic influence of the 24/7 news cycle, the perils of the internet, and the dangers of social media.

In this section, we're taking a broader look at the way that technology more generally may be impacting our stress levels, our pace of living, and our everyday experience of life.

Importantly, the *content* of "digital clutter" is not what makes it so destructive. Instead, what matters is its sheer ubiquity—the fact that there's so much of it, and that it seems to be everywhere.

What portion of *your* stress, unhappiness, restlessness, and life dissatisfaction comes from having to constantly interact with digital clutter?

For example...

- You're trying to have a meal and your phone keeps buzzing with notifications.
- You buy something from an online retailer once and get spam emails from them twice a day every day for the rest of your life.
- You can't seem to ever get any work done because of how many updates and system upgrades your device constantly needs.
- You wake up in the morning and the first thing you do is read work emails, get mad about the headlines, and delete a bunch of random newsletters from people you don't care about.
- You're bombarded with updates from people on social media that you barely remember, and messages from WhatsApp groups you've long stopped participating in.
- Your phone is bloated with countless unwanted apps, and you have a mess of disjointed subscriptions services, poorly

managed passwords, a bad 3 a.m. Reddit scrolling habit, and what feels like a Zoom call every five minutes…

It's exhausting. But it's *not* a mental health issue—it's the very modern problem of too much digital noise, and the overstimulation it can create.

Again, **it's not about *what* you engage with in digital spaces, but the effect that engagement has on you.**

Is it ramping up your cortisol levels and making you irritable?

Is it undermining your close relationships?

Is it depressing you and making you feel disconnected?

Is it eating up time you want to spend on other important things?

Then it doesn't matter what it is—it's got to go.

The problem with digital clutter is that it makes deep, total rest impossible.

It's hard to unplug.

You feel eternally "on call."

Always on, always awake, always wired.

Even if you're not scrolling or reflexively "checking" you phone, you might be *thinking* about it all the same, unable to be present in the moment, and unable to fully relax. The clutter is no longer out there… it's taken over your mental space.

Three Practical Ways to De-Clutter Mentally

Being easily bothered, reactive, and dysregulated often comes down to simply being mentally *cluttered*—i.e., you're just trying to process too much.

Gaining more calm and composure, then, is really about what you *lose*.

To gain more clarity, peace, and flow, you need to adopt the very same strategy you would with a cluttered house: Get rid of the junk, one piece at a time.

Mute the Non-Essentials

Every single time your phone buzzes or pings, your self-contained field of attention is punctured, and it pops like a bubble. Your awareness is hijacked, and you suffer a tiny but powerful moment of amnesia and disorientation.

It then takes effort to recompose yourself and pull your focus back to where it belongs—if you *can* pull it back, that is. More commonly, one disruption tends to bring a few more in its wake:

- Your phone pings
- You check it

- It's nothing
- But now you're already on your phone, so…
- Hey, what's this?
- Within five seconds, you're already a few distractions deep
- Wait, what were you doing again?

Remember that just because a stimulus exists, it doesn't mean you have to respond to it. In fact, it can be liberating to realize that **the digital interruptions in our world are 100% voluntary.** Yes, every single one of them is optional and under our control!

You won't need discipline and effort to keep pulling your attention back to where it belongs if you simply never allow that attention to be pulled away in the first place.

In the digital world, the default setting is for distraction. Digital noise is a given, unfortunately, and so you have to consciously opt out.

Don't waste time trying to wrestle with things that have already forced their way into your field of awareness and disturbed your peace. Instead, make sure that nothing is allowed to disturb your awareness in this way in the first place.

Try this:

- **Turn off notifications.** All of them, or as many as possible. Social media, group chats, and notifications about pointless updates are peace-destroyers and need to be *ruthlessly eliminated*.

- **What about the essential ones?** Adjust your settings so that you are only bothered by incoming calls from people that matter, or from work—provided it's during work hours. If something non-essential is aggressively intruding on your time, consider deleting it completely from your life.
- **Don't "double screen."** One surefire way to splinter your attention and turbocharge your stress levels is to engage simultaneously with two or more devices. It's not multitasking. It's clutter.
- Don't watch a movie while your phone buzzes and flashes on the table.
- Don't game while you're listening to a podcast.
- Don't browse social media while you've got a video call on another tab.
- **Slow down.** Rushing and hurry is a sign of overwhelm, not productivity.
- Don't watch videos or listen to audio at double speed to get through it more quickly.
- Don't skim, browse, or otherwise allow your attention to skip all over the place. Avoid ultra-short media forms that train attention deficit!
- Don't read summaries and crib notes—if something is worth reading, take your time and read the full version.

Create "No-Phone Zones"

The biggest lie of the modern age is that if a certain piece of technology exists, then we necessarily have to use it. If we have a phone, it needs to be close at hand at all times. If TV exists, we need to watch it. If there's a new app to automate a process at work, then you pretty much have no choice but to install that app immediately.

Step back, take a breath and remind yourself that **no tech is always an option.**

You can choose your reaction to:

- Other people's behavior
- Your circumstances
- Everyday emotional triggers

Well, in the same way, you can also practice your own agency when it comes to deciding what technology looks like in your life. You can choose what role technology plays in your life, and how.

Try this: Decide for yourself where in your home you would like to designate a "screen-free" or "phone-free" zone. Each of us has different preferences and tolerance levels, a different way of earning a living, and different priorities, so choose what genuinely makes sense for you. Some potential ideas:

- **Make your bedroom a screen-free zone.** No TV, no devices, no phones of any kind. Checking your phone first thing in the

morning and last thing at night is a one-way ticket to an anxiety-filled day. Instead, read, meditate, or try a calming bedtime ritual.
- **Protect your meals, conversations, and nature time.** Commit to banning phones and devices when you're eating, spending time with people, or out enjoying the natural world.
- **Dare to be bored.** Most of us have trained ourselves to automatically reach for our phones the instant we have a spare moment. Resist this impulse. It's OK to do "nothing." Occasionally, *just sit.* Be quiet and stimulus-free for a while. Let yourself settle. Come away from the algorithms and rediscover what it feels like to generate and direct your own thoughts.

Use Time-Limit Apps

Healthy digital boundaries are not just about keeping gadgets out of your physical space. We also need to place protective barriers and limits around our behavior while we're engaging with tech.

Try this:

- **Set timers.** *Before* you engage, set your intention and draw a line in the sand, timewise. Then stop when the alarm goes off.
- **Example:** Make it a habit that you never turn on a gaming console or sit in front of your

desktop without setting a time limit for yourself. Be firm.
- **Be mindful and be deliberate.** If you enter most digital spaces without a well-defined objective… one will soon be provided for you.
- **Example:** Never pick up your phone without first answering for yourself the question, "What exactly am I doing here?" If you can't properly answer that question, then understand that your desire is likely just a compulsion or addictive impulse. See that urge for what it is and let it pass.
- **Example:** Decide when and how you'll engage with your inbox. You might dedicate a certain daily window period for reading and responding to emails. When the window closes, that's it until the next one!
- **Quickly divert.** Don't just remove digital noise from your life. Replace it with something better.
- **Example:** If you notice yourself engaging with digital noise when you feel bored, alone, or stressed, then make a habit of seeing those urges as helpful cues that you need to reach out to someone, have a conversation, or get outdoors to move your body.

Simplify Decision-Making to Reduce Stress

A high-anxiety life is a *complex* life.

It's the kind of life that's not just bursting with mental clutter, noise, and knee-jerk reactions to relentless emotional demands, but it's also a life **overloaded with possibility.**

In the modern world, we have been conditioned to think of ourselves as choosy consumers, and to see a wide range of options as kind of freedom and privilege.

The truth? This power to choose comes with a cost.

And the more options to choose from, the higher the cost.

Decision fatigue = the mental and emotional depletion that results from excessive decision-making.

Decision fatigue is really *overwhelm* and *overstimulation* by another name.

We have seen that our peace and serenity can be upset by:

- Other people's demands, intrusions, and negativity
- Our own reactivity to triggers like fear or anger
- Digital noise and distraction
- Accumulated daily tensions, stresses, and worries

Options and alternatives can play the same role and disturb our peace of mind just as surely as an insult or an accident can.

Why? Because making decisions requires cognitive and emotional bandwidth—and that capacity is limited.

Decision fatigue is when our available options outstrip our capacity to carefully weigh up those possibilities. Our decision-making faculties can tire and wear out just like a physical muscle can.

Are you decision fatigued?

- You feel irritated and overwhelmed, and you have a short temper when asked to decide something—even if it's something trivial.
- You dread making decisions, including ones that might benefit you, and even procrastinate and avoid the process.
- Sometimes, you can't make a decision at all. You just freeze. You're stuck. You can't think.
- The quality of the decisions you do make seems to decrease, and you find yourself making more careless mistakes.
- You might feel so swamped and overwhelmed that you make rash or impulsive decisions just to get it over with.

If any of this sounds familiar, then you are not necessarily suffering from anxiety, ADHD, or depression. But you are receiving a clear message from your brain: **I am overwhelmed! I have reached my decision capacity, and I can't do it anymore!**

Decision fatigue can lead to poor decisions, which can increase life's complexity... forcing you to make yet more complicated and convoluted decisions.

Round and round you go, reactive and overwhelmed, until you don't want *any* of it, and would prefer to run away and live with the monks in the mountains just for some peace and quiet.

Watch out: The way to overcome "analysis paralysis" and decision fatigue is not to present yourself with yet another choice to make. You cannot choose your way out of choice weariness any more than you can think your way out of overthinking.

There are just two ways to streamline your life and start protecting your limited mental bandwidth (and luckily, you don't have to choose between them!):

1. Increase your bandwidth
2. Decrease your demand on that bandwidth

While it is possible to increase your capacity to process and analyze, this first option offers less scope for improvement than the second. While rest, self-care, and time to recuperate will expand our cognitive bandwidth a little, most of us are already operating at or beyond full capacity. That's why we'll focus more on the second way—cutting down on the number of decisions we have to make.

Remember that resilience is seldom about learning to do more—it's about clearing away what's unnecessary so you can use your existing capacity for what matters most.

Three Practical Ways to Streamline Your Life

Set Daily Defaults

One way to reduce the number of decisions you have to make each day is to make a single decision that will replace many.

Wherever you can, **replace a stressful decision with an automatic habit, a system, or a default**, so you don't have to spend any additional effort. Every decision after that will, in a way, already have been made, so you get to save that precious bandwidth for something else.

Examples:

- **Replace a decision with a habit**. It takes effort and energy to *decide* to go to gym every morning. Instead, make gym-going a habit and stack it alongside your other habits. Make it so that you have to expend effort *not* to go. Arrange for a friend to come and meet you at 6 a.m. every day for the morning run, for example. There's nothing to decide Is it 6 a.m.? Then you run. No decision-making required.

- **Replace a decision with a system**. It takes effort and energy to file your tax return every year, to find money for your tax bill, and to make sure you pay on time. Instead of solving this problem over and over, solve it once, and create a repeatable system or template. That way, you don't have to continually process every step and decision; you've already done all that, now you just follow the system.
- **Replace a decision with a default**. It takes effort and energy to navigate a restaurant menu when you're trying to eat healthily. Instead, decide *once* on a rule, principle, or default that you always follow, no matter what. Then relax. You don't have to make any more decisions. For example, you always order the vegetarian option, you never get dessert, and if you order fries, you only eat half the portion. It doesn't matter what the defaults are, only that their existence spares you from decision fatigue.

Use the "5-2-1 Rule"

Of course, sometimes you really will have to make a decision from scratch.

If a choice really has to be made, try the following rule to streamline the process and save yourself the mental burden.

Step 1: Identify five options, choices, or possibilities.

Step 2: Immediately eliminate three options that are not really speaking to you, narrowing it down to two.

Step 3: Randomly choose between the remaining two—it doesn't even matter which you pick, just pick.

A little further explanation:

- Begin with five choices, no more. There may well be more than five on offer, but realistically, there is not likely to be that much variation in your options that you might miss out by choosing just five. Do this step fairly quickly and without overthinking it.
- In step 2, you are not choosing at all, just eliminating. Does this option light your world on fire? No? Then just scratch it off the list and stop thinking about it.
- Finally, you're on the home stretch—both of your remaining options should be fine, so just pick one.

For example: You're trying to decide on your next audiobook, and you have a few ideas in mind. You quickly compile a short list of five and just forget about the other possibilities for now. You immediately drop one, then after a few minutes decide to get rid of another two that don't seem right for whatever reason (too long, narrator might be boring, whatever).

Finally, you're left with two choices. For extra fun, you toss a coin, make your decision, and move on. No second-guessing.

The beauty of this process is that **it's quick**. It doesn't allow you to get caught up in overanalysis or entertain too wide a range of possibilities. You want to imagine that you're gradually narrowing your range. When you choose five, really choose five and act as though no other options exist in the world. You'll feel calmer.

Caveat: This method is perfect for choosing between meals, TV shows, outfit options, or detergent brands. These are the kinds of everyday decisions that are trivial but can quickly spiral out of control.

Naturally, this process is *not* appropriate for choosing where to live, what job to do, or who to date!

Make Low-Stakes Decisions Fast
Finally, in the spirit of keeping it quick, give yourself a time limit for all those decisions that are small and not ultimately significant. It's these minor decisions that have the biggest risk of wasting your time and trapping you in cycles of indecision.

Try this: Give yourself 60 seconds to make any minor decision. Choosing cereal at the grocery store? Trying to decide what color pajama bottoms to buy? Not sure whether you should sign up for barre or kettle bell class this week?

These things don't matter. Not really.

In fact, wasting precious time and *failing to make a decision* is far worse than just choosing an option—any option. Give yourself 60 seconds, then move on boldly without another thought (hint: That last part may take some practice!).

If you're really struggling, mentally tell yourself that you're not choosing at all—you're just going to try this option *first*, then try something else later. This cuts out any FOMO feelings and tells your second-guessing mind to quieten down.

Summary:

- Stress relief isn't one-and-done. Instead, fill your day with calming micro-activities so you can constantly course-correct and maintain composure.
- Stress can become a self-reinforcing cycle of constant stimulation and over-reactivity. Break the cycle with a breathing reset, a moment in nature, or a few words in a journal.
- The only real solution for everyday, cumulative stress is everyday, cumulative stress-relief. Make stress-management a habit—this is the heart of emotional regulation.

- The world is filled with noise—much of it digital. What matters is not the content, but its effect on you. It can be hard to unplug, but remember that every digital stimulus is voluntary. Slow down, don't multitask, and assert strong digital boundaries.
- Take charge and proactively choose the role tech plays in your life, for example, by creating "no phone zones." Protect your mealtimes, your conversations, and your quite moments in nature. Consider using time-limit apps, site-blockers, timers, or other tools to take back control.
- Simplify your decision-making processes to reduce stress and overwhelm. Cut down on decision fatigue and analysis paralysis by setting automatic and habitual daily "defaults", using the 5-2-1 rule, and making trivial decisions within 60 seconds.

Section 5: Reconcile Yourself With Fear

"To escape fear, you have to go through it, not around it"

- Susan J. Jeffers

Face Panic Instead of Avoiding It

"Courage" has been defined as the quality of mind or spirit that enables a person to face difficulty, danger, pain, etc., *without fear*.

There is, however, something wrong with this definition, and a woman known only as "SM" can show us what it is.

SM is a real person who is literally incapable of feeling fear. She is simply not afraid of anything.

After being diagnosed as a child with Erbach-Wiethe disease, SM suffered brain damage, particularly to the part of the brain responsible for fear recognition, emotional learning, and memory—the amygdala.

Since then, she has lived a life so peculiar that she's been the subject of countless scientific studies. Researchers have described SM as ultra-positive, curious, friendly, and uninhibited, and she appears to experience very few negative emotions.

However, in losing her ability to fear, she also appears to have lost the ability to:

- Read people's emotions
- Accurately tell who is and isn't trustworthy
- Enjoy music
- Understand social cues
- Respect personal space

SM appears to face all life's troubles with zero fear, despair, or urgency—and when it comes to trouble she seems to have faced an unusually high amount.

SM is recorded as having frequently been the victim of crime and abuse, domestic violence, bullying, threats, and being held at gunpoint on one occasion and knifepoint on another.

In fact, it may be precisely her inability to fear that lands her in these difficult situations in the first place. Part of SM's experience seems to come from her impaired threat detection and her resulting inability to protect herself.

It's curious: Without fear, her world is more dangerous.

Now, let's return to our earlier question: Is SM courageous? Is she *brave*?

Few would say so.

Not only does the strange case of SM tell us that **fear is a normal and healthy part of the brain**, but it also tells us how useful it is for our survival.

Importantly, it teaches us something interesting about the nature of courage: **Bravery is not, as they say, the absence of fear, but the ability to feel it, and nevertheless face and overcome it.**

Courage is acknowledging the reality of fear, but recognizing that other things are bigger and more important.

Courage is being afraid to act, but acting anyway.

We began this section on fear with the story of SM because we need to have an accurate and useful understanding of what fear is, how it operates, and what our healthiest and most functional attitude towards it might be.

What is fear?

Fear is the emotional reaction of a normal, healthy physiological response to perceived threat. Fear exists to protect us and promote our survival.

So, what's the problem?

The Stoic Seneca explains it well:

> "Wild animals run from the dangers they actually see, and once they have escaped

them worry no more. We however are tormented alike by what is past and what is to come."

The fear response is there to protect us from real and present danger, and, when that danger subsides, so too should the body's warning alarm. Human beings, however, experience complications to this basic and inbuilt mechanism:

- We fear things that, as Seneca tells us, have already been and gone, or haven't even happened yet.
- We fear things that are completely imaginary and hypothetical.
- We fear things because we perceive them to be a threat, when in reality they aren't.

So, let's put it clearly: The problem is not that we are human beings with a hardwired fear mechanism. **The problem is the misalignment or malfunction of that fear mechanism.**

- Some things in life are dangerous → We should be afraid of them.
- Some things in life may feel scary, but are not dangerous → We should face them.

Really, we are back to the Serenity Prayer again: **We need the wisdom to know when we should face and challenge our fear, and when we should accept it as a normal and self-preserving response.**

In his book 2009 book *Don't Panic*, Reid Wilson explains a key principle in overcoming panic disorders and an unhealthy relationship to fear:

We need to face panic instead of avoiding it.

Your inbuilt threat detection system will sound the alarm whether the stimulus is a wild animal in the bushes (i.e., a genuine threat to your survival) or the thought of making the first move on your crush (i.e., not a threat to your survival in the least).

Facing fears is obviously about this latter kind of fear, not the former—after all, we don't want to turn into SM!

Important: Your inbuilt fear mechanism will *automatically* trigger physical sensations of panic, whether the stimulus is a genuine threat or just a perceived threat. The fear response will kick in so quickly that you won't have a conscious say in the matter.

This is significant: Feeling knee-jerk panic isn't a sign of poor character or low willpower. It doesn't mean you're a coward or doing anything wrong. It just means that *your nervous system is activated.*

What matters is that you have a say in what happens after that response is triggered.

Avoidance might feel like the best strategy. Why? Because when you avoid a stimulus, then you immediately feel better. This relief confirms that the scary thing really was a threat, and that retreating really did save you.

In other words, you reinforce your cowardice.

However, in the long run avoidance only keeps you trapped in fear and subject to it. You never get the chance to prove to yourself that your initial assessment of threat was faulty.

Caving into unfounded fear weakens you and shrinks your world. Avoidance may feel like liberation and comfort in the moment, but it only teaches you to play small and expect little from yourself.

The better strategy? Acknowledge your fear.

Face it.

Be fully present with the reality of your fear.

This breaks fear's hold over you and makes you less reactive, and more resilient.

Best of all, through facing fear you teach yourself something super-important: **Just because your fear response mechanism has been triggered, it doesn't mean that you are necessarily in danger.**

This is the way people become truly courageous.

Three Practical Ways to Face Your Fears

Take Small Exposure Steps

Modern humans seldom face genuine threats to their survival. Instead, our fears are vague, abstract, unfounded, illogical... and sometimes 100% self-generated.

What are *you* afraid of?

- Speaking in public
- Being rejected, judged, or laughed at
- Being alone
- Growing old
- Experiencing strong and unpleasant emotions
- Physical discomfort
- Embarrassing yourself
- Not getting what you want
- Crowds or confined spaces
- Losing or failing
- Hard work, struggle, or adversity
- Being vulnerable, seen, or exposed

There is plenty to be afraid of in this world... but it's never quite as much as the terrors we invent for ourselves.

Healthy fear protects us.

Unhealthy fear limits us.

One of the most important things we can do to reclaim our mental composure and take responsibility for our lives is to discern the difference. We need to be honest:

- Are our fears healthy or unhealthy?
- Are our fears protecting us or constricting us?

If your fear is holding you back in life, then the remedy is to replace avoidance with acknowledgement and acceptance.

Facing fears is not about voluntarily terrifying yourself, however. You can gradually dissolve fear's hold over you with baby steps, and small doses.

For example, you might have had a car accident and now feel terrified of getting back behind the wheel again.

Step 1: Decide that fear doesn't get to determine your behavior—you do. This is crucial. You can't take charge of the situation until you can correctly acknowledge that it's yours to take charge of.

Step 2: Confront what's making you afraid. Expose yourself to it in small, incremental doses.

For example:

- You hang around outside the parked car for a while.
- You sit in the driver's seat, parked, engine off.
- You sit but with the engine idling.

- You do a few laps around the parking lot.
- You drive to the end of the street and back, late at night when there's no other traffic.
- You drive to the end of the street but during the day, when it's busier.
- You drive to the store a few miles away.

You get the picture. The exact steps aren't important. What matters is that you're **gradually ratcheting up your exposure**. Give yourself time to acclimatize to each new task, then take that next baby step.

Important: Don't take the next step until you can feel your anxiety drop at the step you're on. It doesn't have to be zero, but you need to give yourself enough time to teach your nervous system that what you're doing *isn't* dangerous.

Take as long as you need. After completing a "rung" on this "anxiety ladder," pause to reinforce the progress you've made. Celebrate. Tell yourself that you are now no longer a person who is afraid of X.

Allow yourself to update your sense of identity to reflect that.

Stay Put Through the Wave
When fear is triggered, every single cell in your body will want to escape. Run away. Call the whole thing off.

In an instant your mind will generate a million plausible excuses for why you can't carry out the plan you said you would.

Fear will try to convince you: "This feels terrible! It's awful and I hate it! I can't bear it. And it wouldn't feel so bad unless it was really dangerous, right?"

Wrong. We need to learn to consistently push back against the voice of fear:

"I feel anxiety right now, but that doesn't mean I am in danger, or that I'm doing something wrong."

Then sit with it. Stay there. Wait.

The longer you can sit with this fear, the more opportunity you give yourself to prove that, well... nothing happens.

The world doesn't end.

You don't die.

In fact, these powerful, deeply unpleasant feelings of fear rise and then fall again. They don't last forever. The fear comes, then it goes again. If you *stay put*, then you will still be standing after it peaks and then fades.

Remind yourself that escaping at the highest point of your fear will actually reinforce your fear response and teach you precisely the lesson you don't want to learn.

Does the fear feel pretty intense? That's a good thing—it means you're in the peak. And if you're in the peak, then that means that from here on out, that feeling of fear is only going to diminish. *But you have to wait it out.*

Important: Let's be honest, and let's be prepared. Facing your fears won't feel great. It won't feel easy. But anxiety doesn't last forever, and while it's there it won't kill you.

But here's the promise: If you can ride it out *now*, then the next time it appears it will be only half as potent, and the time after that, you will scarcely register it.

Stick it out—it's worth it!

Reframe the Sensations

The fear you feel is real. Fear won't kill you, but it will certainly make its presence known:

- Racing heart
- Ringing ears
- Sweaty palms
- A queasy feeling in the pit of your stomach
- Shallow breathing
- Feeling faint or jittery
- And so on…

Just because the fear isn't a response to a genuine survival threat, it doesn't mean that your nervous system hasn't been activated. That cortisol and adrenaline pumping though your body is real. The sympathetic nervous system response (fight-or-flight mode) is not "all in your head" —it's everywhere in your body.

So, there's no point pretending it isn't.

Instead, try this: Reframe those sensations.

You're sitting behind the steering wheel and your heart is pounding. You're shaking. Every fiber of your being is saying *get out of here*.

Though you can't do anything about these reactions (remember, they're automatic, inbuilt, and lightning fast) you can certainly adjust the way you *perceive* them:

- "I'm experiencing nervous system arousal. My body is in panic mode right now, and there are hormones and neurotransmitters that are creating all these physical sensations I'm feeling."
- "My body is alert. It's responding in this way because it's trying to help me survive."
- "There is nothing bad or dangerous going on in my body. I feel these sensations, but I don't have to be worried about them. I am safe. I'm not in any trouble."

In fact, in some circumstances, you can get really creative with the way you interpret certain body signals:

- **When chatting up your crush.** "That little flutter in my stomach is *excitement*. I'm a

little nervous but also thrilled and enjoying the suspense. I'm enjoying this."
- **When skydiving**. "That jolt of electricity running through my body is *fun*. This is *intense*."
- **When giving an important presentation**. "This shaky, jittery feeling is *energy* and *interest*. I'm so focused right now, and my mind is prepared to act with enthusiasm."

Talk to Panic: Reframe Fear Through Dialogue

Anger and indignation? We don't have to take the bait.

Hurry, demands, guilt, and obligations? We can say no if we want to.

But what about fear? Is it really possible to be unruffled by raw, blind panic?

The answer is *yes*.

Fear has a special hold on the human heart and mind, and it's one emotion that can feel the least manageable, and least under our control.

It makes sense. Fear is a primal emotion with one function: Protect us from threat. The catch, however, is that we are never actually responding to threat, but to our *perception* of threat—and perceptions can be distorted.

Reid Wilson's big idea was this: Anxiety won't kill you. It isn't dangerous and, even though it feels like it at the time, it can't actually hurt you.

What's more, anxiety is not in itself pathological or shameful. Panic—in particular spiraling panic attacks—occur because of our *perception* of our own responses. In other words, **panic becomes a problem when normal anxiety responses are misinterpreted, resisted, or amplified by fear itself.**

Basically, it's not the fear that's scary. It's the fear of the fear!

What does this mean for us?

When there's a potentially triggering stimulus, your brain might detect a threat and respond with fear.

You first instinct—*survive*. Escape. Get away from the scary thing or go to war with it.

You then notice yourself escaping, fleeing, and resisting. And this resistance itself becomes a trigger for yet more fear and resistance.

A fearful response to fear makes fear stronger. When we react this way, we are essentially confirming in our mind that our original perception of the stimulus as scary is correct. We are reinforcing our own helplessness, amplifying the size and seriousness of the threat, and discounting our own ability to withstand and cope.

Is it really possible to be unbothered by fear?

Well, yes and no.

Fear is a biological response. It's an automatic and finely tuned physiological event in the body that has evolved over thousands of years for a specific function. Fear is a neurochemical and hormonal phenomenon, and it's lightning fast. If a giant, hairy spider suddenly appears on your pillow one evening, your response will be 100% automatic!

That said, our response to our inbuilt fear responses is *not* knee-jerk, *not* automatic, and *not* a foregone conclusion.

I might be afraid of speaking in public. Heart pounding, palms sweating, dry throat—my response to that perceived threat is physiological and 100% out of my control. *But what I do with that fear is what matters most.*

Option 1: I decide that my fear is uncomfortable, unacceptable, scary, horrifying, embarrassing, shameful, worrying, inconvenient, or rage-inducing. I judge myself for feeling that fear. I diagnose myself with a condition and condemn myself. I take the fear as a sign that I'm not cut out for public speaking, that I'm doing something wrong, that I'm on the wrong path, that something terrible is happening.

→ Unsurprisingly, I decide to avoid public speaking. Forever.

Option 2: I see the fear and recognize it for what it is: a sensation. Will public speaking actually kill me? Nope. I stand up and speak in public—*even though* my heart is still pounding, my palms are still sweating, and my throat is still dry. I don't die! It's hard, but my fear doesn't get to hijack me. The big surprise is that it's not as bad as I predicted. The next time I talk in public, it's easier. Soon, I wonder what I was ever afraid of in the first place.

→ Over time, I actually come to enjoy public speaking.

Notice something important here. Fear is present in both options. In both options there are sensations, and in both options those sensations are unpleasant. But **the response to fear—whether someone decides to be bothered by these fear sensations or not—that's what makes the difference.**

A more resilient approach is to *talk to panic*. Engage and approach. Treat fear like a passing visitor rather than a dreaded enemy. By dialoguing with anxious thoughts, you strip them of their power and reframe them as temporary, harmless experiences.

This helps build mental toughness because instead of being hijacked by fear, you train yourself to stay calm, grounded, and even a bit detached. By recognizing panic as "just a sensation" and speaking to it directly, you maintain control and reduce its impact.

Three Practical Ways to Get on Top of Fear

Name the Feeling Out Loud

Anxiety hits.

- Your knee-jerk reaction: Run away.
- Your updated, unbothered, and healthier *secondary* reaction: Stay.

When we're fearful, the gut impulse is to flee. Not just from the Scary Thing, but also from the fear itself. Runing away feels like the only way to make the discomfort stop.

The trouble is, **when we escape, we miss out on something else, too. We forfeit something very valuable: the chance to learn.**

When we stay and face fear, we learn:

- What the Scary Thing actually is (i.e., not just what we *think* it is)
- That it is not as big as we thought
- That we are not as helpless as we thought

In other words, by facing fear, we give ourselves the gift of experiencing first-hand a liberating truth: fear passes.

When you run away from fear, all you end up teaching yourself is that escape and avoidance works, and that the Scary Thing really is that bad, that threatening, that un-survivable.

Worst of all, you teach yourself that you are weak.

The understandable first instinct is to escape, but to be truly unbothered, you need to learn to stay. Better still, learn to *engage* and *approach*.

Caveat: Again, if you're facing a literal threat to your survival, be afraid, and flee. That's what *real* fear is for—to alert you to a real threat and help you survive it in a real way. What we're talking about in this chapter isn't real fear—it's fear that arises from the inaccurate perception of threat. *That's* the fear we need to learn to approach and engage. Because that's the only way we can correct that misperception.

Try this: When anxiety rises, calmly say to yourself: "This is just panic. My body is reacting, but I'm safe."

Put a name to what you're feeling. De-mystify it. The world isn't ending, you're just experiencing HPA-axis arousal. You're not dying, your body is just momentarily flooded with stress hormones.

Naming the feeling:

1. Separates you from it
2. Reduces its power over you

Tell yourself, "I'm feeling anxious/hesitant/worried/terrified right now. This situation *feels* dangerous, but it isn't dangerous."

Respond With Calm Phrases

Fear is a magnifying glass. Evolutionarily speaking, fear helps you survive by giving you tunnel vision that forces you to focus on threats.

Read that again. **Fear makes you selectively focus on everything that's going wrong in your world.**

When you're in this state, all your attention will be zoomed in on the problem, the mistake, the danger, the discomfort. All your thoughts will be focused on the negative.

This is not a curious, expansive, problem-solving, receptive, or compassionate state of mind. This is not the kind of mind that is creative, kind, or optimistic. In a very real way, this state of mind doesn't even allow you to *perceive* the positive.

You can gently push against this, though. Just because your first response was panic, it doesn't mean that you can't have a more mindful *secondary* response. Being panicked is OK. But you don't have to continue on in panic.

The moment you become aware, you can choose how you want to talk to yourself.

Try this:

- "You're anxious, but you're not unsafe."
- "You're uncomfortable. And that discomfort will pass, as it always does."

- "Whatever this feeling is, you can handle it."
- "You can be anxious and still do the right thing, right now."
- "Unpleasant feelings can't hurt you. Unpleasant thoughts are not dangerous."
- "This is a problem. And problems can be solved."
- "You don't like this moment, but that's OK, and you're OK."

Once you've calmed down, see if you can gently coax your attention to widen a little and perceive any good things you might have otherwise missed. When you're panicky, everything everywhere feels like a disaster, but is that really true?

Become curious again about those things that are *outside* of your fear tunnel.

Treat Panic Like a Temporary Visitor

When we're trapped in anxiety, our conscious awareness shrinks down to the size of a pinprick, and *now* is the only thing there is—and now feels bad.

It can sincerely feel like the negativity will last forever, and like you'll never feel any another way ever again.

But you will.

Anxiety is never permanent.

No feelings, no matter how heavy or difficult or unbearable they are, last forever.

Remind yourself of this when you're in the thick of a panic spiral. Visualize panic as a guest—an annoying and unwelcome guest, sure—but not a permanent lodger. Anxiety is a visitor you don't necessarily expect or invite, but you can trust that they'll go home eventually!

There's no point getting caught up in an argument with an unwanted guest; that'll only prolong the visit, right? Instead, greet the fear, but then just ignore it. Take the attitude you would towards the random technician coming to read your gas meter:

→ "Oh hey, it's you. OK. Come in. I'm just going to carry on with what I was doing. Please lock the door on your way out."

No big drama. No need to force yourself to be brave or calm.

Just acknowledge, then get on with your life.

The less you resist, the better.

Embodied Poise: Stand Calm to Feel Calm

In the last chapter, we saw that there are really *two* components to the fear response:

1. Your physiological reaction to a perceived threat

2. Your emotional and cognitive reaction to both the perceived threat, and to the physiological reaction itself

Because we can separate these things out, it makes sense to say, "I feel afraid... but I don't *feel* afraid."

- → **People who are easily bothered** and reactive are people whose emotional reactions quickly follow after their physiological reactions.
- → **People who are calm and controlled** are able to experience physiological arousal, but without it taking over their entire mental and emotional experience.

Strong and composed people are able to mentally resist the influence of their physiological fear responses.

While our bodies can influence our thoughts and feelings, the relationship doesn't just go one way: Our thoughts and feelings influence our bodies, too.

In a fascinating 1982 study, Riskind and Gotay found that **physical body posture has regulatory and feedback effects on emotion.**

One study found that when participants were asked to adopt a slouched, slumped posture later developed learned helplessness more readily than participants who were placed in tall, upright, and expansive postures.

Not only did posture seem to impact how people felt, but it also appeared to impact *other people's* perceptions; i.e., observers were more ready to ascribe depression and demotivation to those they saw slouching and slumping.

The authors conclude that **physical posture acts as a cue**—the external posture actually creates genuine internal feelings to match.

Researchers in the field of "embodied cognition" have long noticed, for example, that people don't merely smile because they're happy—they also feel happy *because they smile* (Söderkvist et. al., 2017; Coles et. al., 2022; Mau, 2021).

The smile—a posture of the facial muscles—acts as a cue that triggers matching internal thoughts and sensations: "I guess this must mean I'm happy."

Essentially? It's a fake-it-till-you-make-it scenario.

Or, more accurately, faking it acts as the first step to making it!

Your physical posture influences how you feel.

That means that if you adopt the posture of a person who is:

- Neutral
- Unbothered
- Calm
- In control

Then you are sending yourself a powerful prompt to actually *feel* that way. You become that person.

Adopting a composed physical presence isn't just about "looking calm." There's no fakery involved. Rather, it's about **training your body to help your mind remain unbothered.**

Set up that reinforcing feedback loop: You act calm because you feel calm, and you feel calm because you act calm.

Three Practical Ways to Hold Your Head High… Literally

Pause to Reset Physically

Have you ever seen a terrified dog?

The tucked tail, the hunched spine, the lowered head… this cowering posture is the physiological manifestation of fear. And humans do it too!

If you brace yourself as if for a blow, you will cue your mind to expect that blow. If you shrink and tremble and make yourself small, your body sends your mind the clear message: *It's not safe. Trouble is coming. Protect yourself.*

Instead, the next time you're feeling triggered, pause to consciously:

- Straighten your spine
- Pull your shoulders back
- Lift your chin
- Open up and expand

- Loosen and unclench your jaw
- Stand tall
- Untuck your "tail"!

This sends a completely different message to your brain: *Everything's OK. You're safe.*

In that moment, even if it's very brief, you are neutralizing any stress spikes and cultivating a feeling of steadiness, stability, and control. You can certainly tell yourself verbally, "Everything's OK. I'm safe," but the message may be felt more fully and more immediately if you just go ahead and **physically act as though you are safe**. Your mind will catch up!

- Has someone just told you, "We need to talk"? Consciously take a beath and open your chest, relax, and stand tall.
- Have you just seen a scary-looking piece of mail in your mailbox? Pause, let the tension come out of your shoulders, and relax your jaw. Then open the letter.
- Are you standing around at a party where you don't know anyone? Stand tall. Remember—other people's perceptions are also influenced by your posture. Act calm and composed and they'll treat you that way.

Neutral Posture as Default
You don't have to wait for a fear trigger—adopt a neutral, upright posture as a matter of habit. The more you can carry yourself with physical

poise and uprightness, the easier it will be for your thoughts and feelings to align with that.

You are training your nervous system to default to stillness.

You are setting your baseline—a kind of anchor state that you naturally stay in and fall back into when disturbed.

When life throws something frightening your way, it won't find you already dysregulated or out of balance. Instead, your poise has a kind of *gravity* to it. You stay put. Because neutrality is your permanent, default state, it's just harder to ruffle you.

- **Set your posture every morning**. When you wake up, spend a few mindful moments waking your body up, too. Stand like a person who possesses resilience, character, inner strength, and serenity. Consciously tell your body and mind that *this* state of calm control is your natural state. You'll be more alert to anything threatening to shift you out of that alignment.
- **Practice**. Find moments throughout the day where you can check in your posture and comportment. For example, while in a queue or waiting room, keep your stance open, stand tall, and avoid fidgeting. Don't rush, don't cower, don't slouch. Notice how people treat you with more respect when you look composed.

Mind-Body Checkpoint

Learn to respond *from* stillness and self-control.

When we're reactive, triggered, or unsettled, we tend to respond to stimuli from a place of weakness. We're fielding an attack while unbalanced and on the back foot. As a result, we might lash out, overreact, say something we regret, or unintentionally escalate the situation.

In heated moments, people can "forget themselves" and lose control of the situation. They may quickly become identified with strong emotions, and they may not even realize the runaway feedback loop that is happening between their body and their mind.

Instead, the moment you feel your emotions rising, do a quick body scan.

- How are you standing?
- What are your hands doing?
- What's going on with your jaw?
- How are you breathing?

If you are unbalanced (literally), clenching your fists or jaw, or if any part of you is tight and constricted (including your breath), then you are already well on your way to getting lost in a runaway fight-or-flight response.

Stop!

There is always time to dial things back.

Adjust your posture first → Healthier thoughts and feelings will then come more easily.

Respond from a calm posture.

- A worrying email might throw you off. Find your balance again *first* before typing your response.
- Someone's question or accusation might put you in the spotlight for a moment, and your heart rate may instantly spike. Fix your posture *first*, take a deep breath, and then give your answer.
- An aggressive driver appearing from out of nowhere may give you a sudden scare. *First* pause, readjust your posture, and then decide if it's worth responding at all.

Your mind and body are connected. Check in on what your body is doing, and you will see what your mind is—or will soon be—doing.

Stand Without Crutches

Strong, resilient, unbothered people are those that stand tall, sometimes quite literally.

They have a poise about them, a certain internal sense of self-possession, and unshakeable self-control.

In a very real way, healthy and strong people *hold their own*.

Physically, they demonstrate personal mastery over their bodies with tall, mindful, and upright posture. They are self-contained, well-aligned, and self-sufficient.

Emotionally, they demonstrate the same kind of self-mastery—they are not easily baited or provoked, but are composed, contained, and non-reactive.

Cognitively, they think for themselves, and their arguments and perceptions stand firm on logic and reason, resilient against manipulation or distortion.

As we've seen, being this kind of person is not about being emotionless or never feeling fear. Rather, it's about a willingness to stand on your own two feet... even if sometimes those feet have to walk over steep, uneven, or unstable terrain.

We will end this section with a careful consideration of *fear crutches*—namely, how to avoid them.

What is a fear crutch? It's what fear psychologists like Reid Wilson call "safety behaviors."

Safety behavior = a physical *or mental* action taken to reduce anxiety, or to prevent a feared outcome.

These things are like behavioral or mental lucky charms or superstitions—we believe that if we have/do them, then we will gain a measure of control over the situation, and a little relief over our own anxiety.

What's so bad about that?

Well, in the same way as a crutch makes it easier to walk but doesn't actually teach you to walk more effectively on your own, a psychological crutch feels like it's helping—but really it's preventing you from learning and overcoming your present limits.

Such safety seeking behaviors feel good because they *do* help—in the short-term, anyway. But in the long-term, they just uphold and reinforce our fear.

A safety behavior can be anything:

- Checking locks or switches
- Continually asking for reassurance or getting people to help you
- Carrying a special item like a bottle of water or wearing a certain garment
- Choosing to do an activity in a very tightly controlled way
- Rehearsing, preparations, over-planning, and endless just-in-case schemes
- Always sitting near exits (in case you suddenly need to leave)
- Using substances like drugs or alcohol to cope
- "Research" (i.e., intellectualized rumination)
- Using distraction and denial

- Careful avoidance of things or places that scare you

Example:

You have an irrational fear that one day you will contract a rare form of cancer. This thought becomes a kind of obsession for you; i.e., you are in the habit of bothering and disturbing *yourself*.

But you believe you have a handle on this fear. Every time you feel the panic rising, you quickly go online and seek out some information to put your mind at ease. Maybe you find a new symptom checker, or a little calculator that figures out your estimated risk of rare cancers, given your demographics.

You manage to calm yourself down again, and life moves on... until the obsessive thought appears again, and you start all over.

What's going on here?

- You feel an irrational fear
- You engage in a crutch, or a safety behavior (online research)
- You immediately feel comforted, as though you have protected yourself from the perceived threat

In the short-term, the above process doesn't seem so bad. It's working, right?

But fast forward and look at what happens when one day, for whatever reason, you're prevented from going online to research. You can no longer run through your safety behavior. The result: *You go into a major meltdown.*

The problem? It's got nothing to do with the internet. Rather, the problem is that you are removing the crutch and seeing your situation for what it is: **You are being propped up by a safety behavior that supplies a false sense of security.**

A safety behavior is never a solution—it's more like symptom relief, a hack, a cheat, and a prop. It not only reinforces that the perceived threat really is dangerous, but it also prevents you from ever learning the truth—that the feared outcome is unlikely, and even if it did occur, *you might actually cope.*

Think of it this way: A person only needs to take special precautions for those things that really are threatening and would be unmanageable otherwise. So, every time you lean on your special safeguards, you are only confirming for yourself that these measures are needed—that you wouldn't be able to stand without them.

And that's a lie!

The fact is, we can sometimes deceive ourselves and develop a dependency on certain behaviors (internal or external) that are not true resilience or coping—they are actually *getting in the way* of you learning true resilience and coping.

Example: You're a performer, but you suffer badly from stage fright. Your "solution"? Being ultra-prepared. As long as you get to the venue first, rehearse for hours, do sound checks in a very, very specific way, then choose exactly where you'll stand... then you're fine.

All hell breaks loose, however, if this pre-show ritual is disrupted!

The truth is that the safety behavior is really just a red herring—it doesn't keep you safe any more than Dumbo's magic feather helps him fly!

Safety behaviors are just band aids, but they are band aids that actually stop wounds from healing. Ditch them so you can *engage fully and productively* with fear, instead.

We've already seen that escape and avoidance only reinforce fear's power over you. But we can escape and avoid in clever, hidden ways.

Remember: True resilience comes from gradually dropping illusory training wheels and safety nets so you can prove to yourself that *you can handle discomfort without them.*

Three Practical Ways to Drop Your Psychological Crutches

Identify Your Safety Behaviors

Naturally, you can't let go of a safety behavior if you don't even know you have it.

How do you identify something that may be hiding, hard to spot, or even masquerading as healthy, resilient behavior?

It can be tricky because *safety behaviors often feel great*—they bring relief and a sense of control and protection.

How to identify your fear crutches

Step 1: Think carefully (and honestly) about what scares you, and when last you felt afraid or anxious about it.

Step 2: Reflect on this fear, and how you dealt with it at the time. Let's say you felt panicked and anxious at work yesterday. You were feeling antisocial and awkward, and, on reflection, you realize that you wore your headphones to "protect" you—i.e., to discourage people from trying to talk to you.

Step 3: A single behavior is just a single behavior. Instead, keep on the lookout for behavior *patterns*. Do you often use your headphones this way? What else might you be doing to avert social interaction? Perhaps you unconsciously avoid eye contact? Use closed body language as a shield?

Step 4: If you're not sure whether something is a safety behavior, consider what happens after you engage in it. Quick, short-term relief in the moment suggests you may be dealing with a fear crutch.

Important: A safety behavior could theoretically be anything—it's not *what* you're doing, but *why* you're doing it, and the role that behavior is playing in your life.

If it's a subtle way to avoid your fear, it could be a safety behavior—even if that behavior is ordinarily considered healthy and normal. Wearing headphones, for example, is a neutral activity that someone could engage in without feeling anxious or avoidant.

Test Your Assumptions With Small Exposures
You're not trying to quit a bad habit cold turkey. Instead, frame the exercise as an *experiment*. Wait for a low-stakes situation and try going without your crutch in a small way. Then simply observe what happens.

Do you feel anxiety ramping up a little?

Watch that anxiety and see how it unfolds over time.

Recall the process of taking intentional baby steps towards your fear. More than likely, if you *stay with* anxiety, it peaks... but eventually subsides again. Congratulations! You've proved to yourself that you're just fine without your safety behavior.

- You might observe that you're reaching for your headphones automatically.
- Notice this impulse.

- Notice yourself choosing to consciously resist it.
- Notice your discomfort increasing a little.
- Notice it petering out again.
- Then notice that nothing else happens.

This entire process could last just a few seconds. But it's a data point! And it disconfirms your existing hypothesis that your headphones are a necessary part of staying safe in the world.

Often, when fear has a hold over our lives, we hold a deep, three-part core belief:

"A bad thing is going to happen, and when it does, it's going to be absolutely terrible, and I won't be able to stand it/bear it/cope with it."

Let's break this down, and try to see things in a more balanced way:

- **A bad thing will happen** – Is this true? Is it 100% certain? The bad thing often doesn't happen. Sometimes, a good thing happens instead. Have you spent time considering the best-case scenario, too?
- **It's going to be really, really terrible** – Is this true? Negative outcomes are a fact of life, but is every negative outcome automatically the worst it could be? Might the outcome be something mild—like momentary embarrassment, a little discomfort, or a slight disappointment?

- **I'm not going to manage** – Is this true? Fear and anxiety can make us feel totally helpless and at the mercy of external events. But haven't you survived difficult, scary, or unpleasant things before? Isn't it true that you have some strengths and resources to draw on to help you survive and get through the worst possibility, should it come to pass?

Small exposures are like lessons. They teach you that when you face your fear:

- Sometimes nothing bad happens
- If the bad thing *does* happen, it's often not as bad as you predicted
- Even if it *is* bad, you are actually way stronger than you give yourself credit for!

You can only learn these things, however, when you throw away the crutches.

Celebrate Your Progress

Every time you face your fear without safety behaviors, pause and acknowledge that win. Record each success and monitor your progress over time. You are gathering proof that things can change, and for the better.

The next time you face something scary and seemingly insurmountable, you may be tempted to think, "I can't do this. I'm not strong enough." But take a look at your records and you'll discover plenty of evidence to the contrary—you can do it, because you've done it before!

Be proud of your growing mental strength. Watch yourself changing gradually over time. Every time you "survive" you build courage and faith in yourself—and that's what resilience is made of.

Summary:

- The fear response is a normal, protective physiological response, but unhealthy fear is the malfunction of this mechanism. Unhealthy fear restricts us. A fearful response to fear strengthens that fear; instead, approach, engage, and dialogue with that fear.
- Healthy fear protects us, but unhealthy fear needs to be acknowledged and faced directly. Avoidance only reinforces fear. Bravery is not the absence of fear, but the decision to overcome it for the sake of something more important.
- Take small exposure steps to gradually confront fears and master them. Stay put through the wave. Physical anxiety symptoms are real—but you can reframe them in a more beneficial way.
- When anxiety hits, name the feeling out loud, accept it as a temporary sensation, and remain instead of fleeing. Expand and redirect your attention with calming phrases.
- Adopt a relaxed, upright, and expansive posture to cue your mind to feel calm. Set a

neutral posture as your default and regularly check in with your body throughout the day to adjust and correct. Respond from stillness, not fear or imbalance.

- Stand on your own two feet without physical or mental crutches. Identify and drop safety behaviors that are keeping you stuck. Ditch psychological band aids and props and engage with your fear directly. Experiment with small exposures and celebrate your progress.

Section 6: Become Unbaitable

"Attachment is the great fabricator of illusions; reality can be obtained only by someone who is detached."

- Amir Levine

Handle Criticism With Logic, Not Emotion

Life is filled to the brim with noise and nonsense. Have you noticed?

Yet somewhere in that noise and nonsense there is something else: information that is true and useful.

Throughout life, you will encounter:

- Other people's (plentiful) opinions and problems
- Distractions and clutter of all kinds
- Outright deception, manipulation, and exploitation
- People's judgments and appraisals of you
- Criticism, poor treatment, and hostility
- Accidents, setbacks, and inexplicable adversities

- Embarrassments, rejections, and disappointments
- Daily stresses, snags, problems, and complications
- A whole universe's worth of ideas, images, ideologies, arguments, perspectives, stories, concepts, beliefs, and rabbit holes that may or may not lead you to where you want to go

Somewhere in all this, however, is genuinely valuable feedback, correction, wisdom, instruction, encouragement, and knowledge. Somewhere in there is truth, and reality.

Signal and **noise**, mixed up together.

We are thus faced with a problem:

- If we are too reactive, too hooked into external stimuli, and too unstable, we are weak to the noise: We are easily manipulated, disturbed, distracted, and distressed.
- We suffer because of *too much noise.*
- On the other hand, if we are 100% impenetrable, unshakeable, unfazed, indifferent, and in complete control of our own emotions, then we are at risk of detaching in an unhealthy way, and losing touch. We lose humility, receptiveness, and curiosity.
- We suffer because of *too little signal.*

Your goal is not to "learn to act like nothing bothers you."

It's not to be unflinching, numb, or unmoved. Rather, it's to **become discerning.**

For a third time we encounter the spirit of the Serenity Payer—**what we need most is the wisdom to know the difference between signal and noise.**

The ability and willingness to **respond to signal and ignore noise.**

To become truly masterful at your own self-regulation, it's not about caring less—it's about caring more wisely.

Trying to be in control, seeing your mind as a weapon or as armor against other weapons, and framing your experience in terms of war, power, and force—these things are all *incredibly stressful*.

Plus, they seldom work.

Instead, become unbaitable by changing your frame:

You're not an unmovable, muscly Stoic warrior in a video game. You're a *scientist*.

You're an observer.

Your mind is a scalpel, not a sword, and certainly not a hammer.

There is no battle raging all around you—only data, some of which may be useful to you.

Don't bother with the bluster and heroism of emotional detachment—instead, use your bandwidth to become more emotionally *discriminating*. **The person with overly rigid boundaries and a fear of feeling is just as controlled by external forces as the person who is unstable and emotionally reactive.**

Think of it this way: Whether you're pushing or pulling, you're attached. If you're forcefully resisting or desperately clinging, you're still hooked in, and that experience is controlling you.

There's a third option. Stand a little way off to the side of the experience and merely observe. Then choose your response. *This* is what self-mastery looks like. This is real detachment.

Emotional reactivity is weakness and dependency—but so is being emotionally shut-down.

- Don't suppress emotions—choose which ones you're going to give power to.
- Don't react, respond.
- Don't shut down, focus.

Be emotionally dynamic and flowing, but let that flow move over the solid bedrock of your own sovereignty. When you have clarity of purpose and stand on your own two feet, you engage with the world in a strategic, not chaotic way. But you *do* engage with it.

The world is filled with noise, but we are the ones who decide what gets through, when, and why. **We become filters, not walls.** This is freedom.

One amazing side effect of adopting this mindset is other people's response to you. They will sense that bedrock of sovereignty beneath your flexible surface and will respect it. They may even start to respond to you not as something to be moved, but something around which *they* must move.

Remember:

- You don't have to be liked, approved of, or validated by anyone.
- Most of it is noise—it's transient and doesn't ultimately matter.
- You don't *have to* react—to defend, retaliate, convince, or prove yourself.

So what do we do when we encounter setbacks, criticism, or negative feedback? How do we become effective filters?

Three Practical Ways to Sift Through the Noise

Flat out insults?

There's nothing to think about or analyze—you can just move swiftly on. The less you think about it, the better.

Random attacks, accidents, and rudeness can be similarly dismissed. These things don't mean anything, and you only waste time and energy trying to uncover a meaning.

But there's one area worth our more careful discernment: criticism and negative feedback from others.

For example:

- Your boss has delivered some harsh words about your work.
- Your close friend has shared strong misgivings over a decision you're making.
- A stranger on the internet has commented that your face is stupid.
- Your mother has criticized your driving.
- Your partner dislikes your freckles.

You've probably faced dozens of incidents exactly like this (hopefully not all in one day). How do you sort through this and mine out the value?

Pause Before Responding

Reactivity is fast and impulsive. It's knee-jerk because it's really part of the physiological fear response.

Responsiveness is slower, because it takes time to carefully and intentionally consider a stimulus.

Force yourself to pause and find your center. Count to three if it helps.

Whatever you do, don't abandon your emotional sovereignty, or let your attention or energy be hijacked. Notice the urge to lash out, protect yourself, argue, or sink into self-pity and shame. Find the gap—that little space where you choose your response. Choose to be still for a moment.

Picture this: You are a king or queen in a castle over which you have complete dominion. *You* decide whether a messenger can enter your royal courts, and you decide whether or not to give them an audience. Even if a messenger comes in kicking and screaming, or declaring war, you sit calmly on your throne and *first just consider.*

In this kingdom, you don't rule over other people—instead, your own impulsive reactions are your subjects. So, tell them to stand down while you consider the matter carefully.

Try this:

Ask a few questions.

- Does this feedback or criticism hold a grain of truth in it?
- Could this feedback or criticism help me to learn, improve, or grow?
- Ego aside, is the message I'm hearing fair, accurate, or useful in any way?

- Does this feedback or criticism pertain to something I genuinely have control over?

If you can honestly answer *no* to all the above questions, then you can safely ignore this criticism.

- Somebody labelling you a Nazi? No grain of truth → dismiss.
- Somebody judging your taste in music? Who cares—this feedback is not something that can help you learn or grow → dismiss.
- Somebody accusing you of something you didn't do? Not fair or accurate → dismiss.
- Somebody mad at you for the traffic? That's not something you have control over → dismiss.

Granted, these kinds of criticisms are easy to dismiss. It takes a lot more courage and presence of mind to seriously reflect on feedback and take it on board.

Consider a few other principles:

Sort Feedback by Source
It's not entirely true to say that other people's opinions don't matter.

Some do, some don't. In fact, a lot of the time, other people's opinions are neither here nor there, and we ourselves are not required to form an opinion about them.

We need to pay attention to the opinions of people that count. Who are they?

- People who you respect and admire.
- People who have legitimate expertise, authority, or knowledge.
- People who share your goals and/or values.
- People who have successfully achieved what you wish to achieve.
- People who are walking your path.
- People you have made promises or commitments to, those who depend on you, or those to whom you owe an obligation.

It goes without saying that *your* opinion of yourself matters, too!

Everyone's a critic, as they say, but only a few people in your life are critics that matter. **Consider the source of the criticism, not only who it's coming from, but *why* it's coming from there**. You'll need to be a little shrewd, but also intellectually honest with yourself.

Example:

Consider the criticism: "Your new business venture is a bad idea. You're rushing it and taking on too much risk."

Should you dismiss this or not? That depends on where it's coming from.

- A business expert with experience in your field?

- A close friend with an unusually risk-averse personality?
- Your mom who loves you to death but doesn't understand your line of work?
- A potential business rival?
- The trading standards authorities?

Sometimes we can determine the validity of a criticism by its content alone; other times we have to take a close look at the *source* of the criticism. As you can see above, people may be moved to comment, judge, or criticize from reasons and motivations that have *nothing to do with you and your best interests.*

Your job is to carefully decide what's what.

If you're ever in doubt about this, consider how often you yourself criticize people because you're a little jealous of them, because you're projecting your own fears or values onto them, or simply out of habit. How many careless remarks have you made that, when it comes down to it, you don't really *mean*?

If someone's criticism doesn't come from an informed place of wanting to help you improve, then don't take it that way. Take it for what it is: noise.

Reframe Criticism as Data
Life gets much, much simpler when you agree with yourself that you will not take things

personally. Even and especially things that are meant personally!

Instead, treat comments—good ones, bad ones, neutral ones—as information only.

Filter them according to the potential value they bring to your life, not according to how they make you feel.

Tell yourself:

- Other people's comments, judgments, criticisms, and opinions about me do not define me.
- Fair and constructive negative feedback is not a personal attack or something to be ashamed of. It's not something to be proud of, either. It's a mere fact of life, and one to engage with calmly.
- Making mistakes, falling short, being called out, being wrong, being corrected, or even being disciplined are not the end of the world. Wisdom happily receives instruction. Foolishness prefers its own way.

Some data you receive may be mixed or distorted – A person might make a rude and personally-motivated criticism of you, for example, but their general observation about you may be perfectly sound. What then?

Take the truth, and disregard the way that truth was delivered. That person can be an enemy— but they've still done you a favor.

If you're feeling hurt or attacked, realize that your most powerful move is not to go into prideful denial nor is it to fall back into victimhood. Instead, criticisms lose all their sting when you look at them as tools, information, insight, and fuel for growth.

Use them like a sculptor uses tools—some will help your refine your masterpiece, others can be tossed aside.

Whether you accept or reject an incoming criticism, there's no point taking any of it personally or getting emotional.

Tell yourself:

- I am not interested in nor distracted by the trivial.
- I invest my energy where it will bring me the best return.
- The remedy for caring too much about the wrong things is to care more about the right things.
- I don't need to fight, negotiate, persuade, analyze, prove, or ask for permission or validation.
- In the face of criticism, I don't crumble—I assess. I keep what is constructive and let go of what isn't.

You *will* be criticized in life. Face it rationally and with poise. Here's the big secret: You can grow and develop and improve *without* shame, judgment, fear, or ego.

Thought Labeling: Observe, Don't Get Hooked

There is a lot of worthless noise out there in the world—but there's also a lot of noise *in here*, inside our own minds.

Some of us are masters at ignoring the provocations of others, and yet we relentlessly provoke *ourselves*, never quite realizing what we are doing, or indeed that we can stop. Basically, **we bother and upset ourselves** every time we treat our own thoughts as though they are:

- Commands
- Absolute objective truth
- Permanent

The truth?

Thoughts are just thoughts.

They're electrochemical flutters in your brain. They arise and then they fall away again. Some of them are useful, some not. Some are conscious, some are lazy, automatic, and habitual. Some are true and others are bald-faced lies. *Most* are just noise, fluff, distraction, and nothingness.

Unbothered people have all the same thoughts that bothered people have—what differs is the *relationship* they have to their own thoughts.

Action and Commitment Therapy (ACT) is a therapeutic approach that combines mindfulness with CBT principles. The idea is to cultivate *psychological flexibility*, which is the ability to face difficult thoughts and feelings head on, without resistance or escape. From a more accepting vantage point, you can take conscious action towards the goals that matter, according to your values (*Acceptance and Commitment Therapy: An Experiential Approach to Behavior Change,* Hayes et. al., 2011)

One of the six core principles in ACT is **cognitive defusion.**

Let's take a closer look.

To fuse = to join or blend something into a single whole.

If we are fused with our thoughts, then we are so bonded and merged with them that we are indistinguishable from them. In other words, we become our thoughts.

This is way, way worse than being merely *bothered* by our thoughts—this is being completely overtaken and governed by them. It's more than being influenced by thoughts, it's being defined by them.

> ➔ The result is reactivity, mindlessness, stress, and dysregulation.

There's an antidote: Cognitive **de**fusion is about separation and creating a little more psychological distance. It restores a healthier attitude towards those electrochemical flutters in your brain and puts you back in charge.

ACT has many different techniques for bringing about this therapeutic separation, but one especially useful approach is *thought labeling.*

Thought labelling is powerful but simple. It helps us to see that:

- Thoughts are not facts
- Thoughts are not permanent
- Thoughts are not commands

To label a thought, we simply call it by its name. We give it a label:

"You are a thought."

When your head is twisted up in anxiety spirals, it feels like the world itself is twisted up. You are completely caught up in and identified with that distress. You may completely lose sight of everything else—it's as though you always felt the way you feel right now, and you're sure you always will.

You are inside the storm.

You might say, *from this place of fusion*: "Life is horrible and crazy. There's no point going on. I hate this. I give up."

But what happens when you step a little outside of the storm? What happens when you can appreciate the storm *as a storm?*

When you label this experience, identify the thought and give a name to what's happening, it instantly makes it separate from you.

Compare:

- "Life is horrible and crazy."
- "Right now I'm having the thought that life is horrible and crazy."

You can instantly see which one feels a little more manageable!

When you detach and see thoughts for what they are, they suddenly don't seem so big and overwhelming. So permanent. So personal.

The storm is still happening, yes, but you're *outside* it now, perhaps watching it unfold a little way off on the horizon.

When there's emotional distance, there's the opportunity to act on your thoughts—and that means that you have options for self-regulation. Unbothered people understand how to do this naturally; they have all the same thoughts and feelings that anyone else does, only *they are not standing so very close* to those experiences.

Three Practical Ways to Be Bigger Than Your Thoughts

Quiet Labeling

Thought labelling takes a little practice and a lot of self-awareness.

Once you are already upset and emotionally hooked, it will only get harder and harder to recognize what's going on and pump the breaks. One way to acquire the habit of distance and defusion is to practice a little when you're calm and mindful.

Try this:

A simple five-minute mediation whenever you have a moment can work wonders.

- Take a few deep breaths, close your eyes, and find your center.
- Calmly and without judgment **notice** whatever floats into and out of your mind. You are not forcing, resisting, or controlling anything. You're just becoming aware of what is already unfolding.
- Give each thought a little label:
- "I'm noticing that I'm feeling bored."
- "I am aware of my thoughts racing right now."
- "I'm observing my thinking."
- "I am wondering about work and money."
- Even a simple label will do the trick: "Anxiety." "Impatience is happening."

It's important that these are neutral labels—you are not judging, condemning, or even interpreting your experience, like this:

- "I'm noticing that I'm messing up again."
- "I'm aware of just what a basket case I am."
- "I'm being triggered because of my old attachment trauma."

These are not useful labels. They're just self-criticism disguised as mindfulness. But even this is OK if that is indeed what arises in your field of awareness:

"I'm noticing myself making judgments. I'm aware of how I'm analyzing and interpreting."

See how that works? That's the beauty of thought labelling—no matter what your experience is, putting a label on it will help you gain a little distance and regain your emotional anchoring.

Remember that there is no big puzzle to solve, and you're not trying to play gotcha with your own mind.

You're just gently making a perspective switch.

Visualization Practice

In ACT, there are plenty of helpful metaphors that make it easier to achieve that all-important perspective shift. You can include them in your daily meditation practice, or just keep them in mind when you notice that you're feeling triggered:

- **Clouds in the sky.** If you notice yourself anxiously scrabbling after every thought (and your thoughts are going a thousand miles an hour) try this visualization. Your mind is the clear, calm, depthless blue of the sky. Your thoughts are like weather—like clouds. They pass over, but they don't permanently change the character of the sky underneath, which is eternal, and eternally calm. You're the sky, not the clouds.
- **Leaves on a stream.** Visualize yourself sitting beside a gently flowing stream. When a thought pops into your head, imagine just gently placing it on a leaf floating by on the stream. Watch the stream carry the thought away. Whatever the thought is, put it on a leaf, and watch it go by. Your conscious awareness is the stream. Thoughts come, and they go again. Let them.
- **Unruly passengers on your bus.** Imagine that you are driving a bus. You have a crowd of passengers onboard—one is barking orders, another is drunk, another is crying and having a panic attack, and several are arguing with each other about which way to go. These passengers are your thoughts and emotions. But *you* are the driver, and *you* decide where the bus goes. Don't let them take the wheel and crash the bus! If they're

not helping, tell them to take a seat and behave.
- **Trains leaving the station.** You're sitting on a bench at the train station. Trains are coming into the station and leaving again, and each one has a sign at the front announcing its destination. A train can arrive at the station, but that doesn't mean you have to get on board. It's the same with thoughts and feelings. "Rage", "Despair", and "Distraction" may all pull up, but is that where you want to go? If not, stay put and let the train go. Just because a thought emerges, it doesn't mean you have to grab a hold of it and follow it to its fullest conclusion.

Use a Journal

One way to firmly put distance between yourself and intense thoughts is to do so literally—in a journal.

Try this:

When you're feeling overwhelmed and overidentified with what's whizzing around in your head, pause for a moment and reach for a journal.

Now, do a "brain dump" and put everything that's *in* your head *out* of your head. You can do this with a few keywords or phrases, in full sentences or even in symbols and pictures if that feels right.

Take your time and keep going until you feel that there's nothing more to say; i.e., you're just repeating yourself. Putting your thoughts into words will immediately create psychological distance and make overwhelming experiences seem more manageable.

But you may wish to take things even further:

- Tear the paper or crumple it up, then throw it away.
- If you like, burn it!
- Set the paper off to one side. You're here, it's over there.
- Create a "worry journal" ritual—once a thought is put in a journal and the cover closed, you don't have to carry it anymore.
- Fold up the paper and make it physically small. See how trivial it is. See how it's literally something you can pick up or put down again.

Finally, one unexpectedly effective way to use thought labelling is to bring in a little humor and irreverence.

When we are tightly fused with our thoughts, everything can feel so incredibly *heavy*. Want to gain a little psychological distance? Simply refuse to take these things that seriously.

This drains thoughts of their power.

Try this: Use a little playful mockery to cut worries down to size.

Example: Give your negative thought patterns a ridiculous persona, complete with undignified name. For example, your inner critic can be recast as a fat little cartoon blob that is more comical than threatening:

"Oh hi, Fat Neville, it's you again. Yes, yes, I'm sure you have something very important to tell me, but can it wait? I'm busy with something important here."

Emotional Distancing: Become a Witness, Not a Reactor

In a paper titled, "Making meaning out of negative experiences by self-distancing", Kross & Ayduk (2011) discuss a fascinating phenomenon they call the **Self-Reflection Paradox.** It goes like this:

People believe and are often told that *reflecting on negative experiences* can help them to process and heal, and eventually improve their emotional regulation. This is why, for example, people are told to try therapeutic role play or creative writing exercises.

However, there's a catch: The clinical evidence actually suggests that reflection can make things worse.

While you're trying to understand why something happened and pick it apart, you risk slipping into rumination and may end up amplifying and dwelling on all the problems you're trying to solve.

Kross and Ayduk claim that not all forms of reflection are created equal, and so they asked the question: What kind of reflection helps? And what kind of reflection makes things worse?

They concluded that there are at least two types:

1. Self-immersed reflection
2. Self-distanced reflection

Self-immersed reflection: This means revisiting and re-experiencing a negative emotion from a first person, "through my eyes" perspective.

- The focus: immediate feelings and concrete facts
- The result: increased rumination, emotional escalation

Self-distanced perspective: This means regarding past events from a more detached and cognitively defused position—a "fly on the wall" perspective.

- The focus: contextual information, broader meanings, and reappraisals of what happened and why
- The result: emotions are actually processed and released

Reflection alone, then, is not necessarily helpful. **It's the *way* we reflect that matters.**

When you see events in your life from a self-distanced perspective, you are looking at the same content, but the kind of thoughts you're having about that content are very different.

Many "overthinkers" are not overthinking at all—but the *kind of thoughts* they're entertaining are not helpful.

Self-immersed reflection leads to rumination.

Self-distanced reflection stops rumination—and mobilizes the mind to take healthy, conscious action.

It's the distance that allows you to **process**—not **get stuck.**

Three Practical Ways to Change Your Perspective

Narrative Framing

Humankind has been processing emotional content via stories since the dawn of time.

A story is a neat and intuitive way to provide a little cognitive defusion, but it's so much more than that. The frame you put around a story—the way you tell it—can drastically alter the way you feel about it, and what you do next.

A story helps you reflect emotionally, but it doesn't stop there. A story's **narrative drive always keeps it moving**—a story goes somewhere, it works itself out, and the emotions it stirs up are processed, digested, and converted into something useful. That's the power of narrative.

How can you use this power to take control, broaden your perspective, and dial down emotional intensity?

- **Change the tense.** It may seem a little obvious, but when you talk to yourself about difficult experiences, *use the past tense*. Placing an experience in the past puts a natural limit on it—in fact, it shows that it's already been and gone. Present tense means the trouble is ongoing... and who knows how long for? Note the difference:
- "The crowds out here today are insane, there are so many people here I'm losing my mind."
- "A lot of people came out today. I didn't expect such a big crowd. I lost my temper back there."
- **Switch your focus.** The art of rhetoric is the skill of using words to influence. But there's one very important person it allows you to influence: yourself! A narrative is in fact a perspective—a pair of glasses through which you view reality. By changing the words you use, you alter your focus... and the whole story changes.
- **Consider how your word choice influences your frame.** Instead of calling something a problem, disaster, or crisis, call it a challenge. What happens, for example, when you call it a "snag"? Instead of talking

like life is *punishing* you, see what happens when you frame it as *teaching* you.

- **Take the longer view.** Narratives are never single events—they're strings of events. These events gain their meaning in context, relative to one another. We don't mind when the hero has a setback, for example, because we know that he's just temporarily in the hard part of the story—and the good part is coming. Learn to frame your own life this way.
- **Put things in context.** You're not "a failure." You've failed now, with this one thing, this one time. Zoom out so you can see all the successes that came before, and all the successes that are still possible. See this event as just *one beat* in the story.
- **Find the meaning.** A love story is all the sweeter because the lovers are separated for a little while. How can you make meaning of your own adversities and troubles? "At the time I thought my world was ending, but now I can see that, in a way, it needed to end… so that I could create something better."

Third-Person Shift

Authors choose to write in first- or second-person voice (for example "I jumped" or "You laughed") for good reason—it makes the story feel more immediate, more relatable, and more personal. In other words, it helps you to *fuse* with what's happening on the page.

For precisely these reasons, we need to do the opposite!

By using third person voice ("He said" or "Jane asked") you take on the perspective of an observer who is watching at some distance. This creates a psychological buffer.

The emotion is no longer yours—it's his, or Jane's.

It's no longer a part of your permanent identity, but a passing experience, out there in the external world.

You are no longer a participant in the story, but a witness and an observer. The stakes are immediately lowered.

By making this simple perspective switch, you:

- Reduce intensity and overwhelm
- Gain more clarity
- Enhance your reasoning and understanding of a situation
- Reduce your chances of being baited, hooked, provoked, or distracted

The third-person voice is a great *neutralizer*. How can we use this more distanced voice in ordinary life?

- When reflecting on a stressful or unpleasant experience, simply tweak your language:
    - Not: "I am having a hard time."

- o But: "He is having a hard time."
- o Not: "I might get fired."
- o But: "The employee may be fired."
- Another possibility is to **switch to passive voice** and remove the subject of a sentence entirely. This also introduces more neutrality and distance:
  - o Not: "You're arguing with me."
  - o But: "There is a disagreement."
  - o Not: "You lost the money."
  - o But: "The money was lost."

Step Back Before Responding

Try this: When you find yourself in a distressing, unexpected, or difficult situation, take a step back—physically. If that's not possible, you can just imagine yourself adding that tiny bit of physical distance.

It sounds insignificant, but there really is value in prompting yourself to quite literally take the bigger view—something you can only do from further away.

Pausing and stepping back is a way to **gain positional or physical distance.**

- If an intense situation feels like it's spiraling out of control, remember that you can remove yourself where possible.
- Imagine yourself standing outside of the situation, even looking down on it from above. You'll feel calmer and you'll think more clearly about what's unfolding.

- Combine the third person shift with physical distance: Imagine you're watching an event or conversation unfold on a TV screen.

You can also find creative ways to bring in a little **temporal distance**, i.e., separate yourself in time.

- If someone has made a sudden demand on you, ask for a little time to think it over and get back to them. Never rush yourself or allow yourself to be rushed.
- Plan important or stressful events for a time when you won't feel pressured or distracted. Give yourself plenty of buffer time on either side of emotionally demanding appointments or tasks.
- Wait it out. Sometimes, the only thing that makes intense emotions feel more manageable is to sleep them off and let the dust settle. Re-evaluate once you're rested and you've had time to clear your head.

Summary:

- In a hyper-stimulating world, become discerning: Learn to tune into the signal and ignore the noise. Don't push or pull—both are forms of attachment. Instead, care, but care wisely. Become a filter, not a wall.
- When given criticisms or negative feedback, always pause before responding. Consider the source and the purpose and reframe the

- message as data you can use to improve and grow. Dismiss the rest.
- Thought labeling allows you observe your own thoughts and emotions without getting hooked and controlled by them. Notice your thoughts without judgment or interpretation. Defuse from thoughts by seeing them as thoughts.
- Use visualization to imagine thoughts arising and passing again and reconnect to your ability to stand apart from that flow. Journaling and putting thoughts into words can also help create psychological distance—literally.
- Self-distancing reflection will help you become a witness to your thoughts and emotions, not a reactor to them. Avoid self-immersed reflection (i.e., rumination and dwelling).
- Adjust your perspective by changing the narrative, shifting into third person, and literally altering your posture and position in space. More distance = a broader perspective = better emotional regulation.

Conclusion

We've covered a lot of ground—congratulations for making it this far!

By the time you reach the final page of this book, my sincere hope is that something has subtly shifted. That a change has occurred... not in the world out there, *but within you.*

Bother is a part of life. People are sometimes rude, things don't always go to plan, and the daily conveyer belt of stresses, hassles, insults, injustices, and annoyances shows no signs of slowing down.

And yet when you have mastered the skill of self-regulation, when you know deep within your bones who you are and what you stand for, when you have courage and can stand firm in your convictions, and when you have made a conscious decision to orient towards peace and simplicity—then none of that other stuff matters.

It just stops mattering.

The wonderful thing about being unbothered is that you are no longer dependent on external circumstances. **Your life is no longer conditional.**

You are serene because you have determined to be that way, and it doesn't matter one bit what the world is or isn't doing all around you.

There is no peace or ease more unwavering than this.

Let's recap:

Perception matters. Choose not to be a victim. Choose not to be passive.

We cannot control life, but we have perfect sovereignty when it comes to choosing our reaction to it. You decide where to put your attention, energy, and time. Claim your power and responsibility to do so, and anchor in your own purpose, not the short-lived demands of others.

Be intentional.

Be conscious.

Be calm.

It's OK to have limits, to have preferences, and to be different. It's OK to turn away from the unimportant for the sake of the important. It's

OK to point towards what matters—and ignore the rest.

Your first act of free will is deciding where to place your attention.

Focus on the positive:

- The people and ideas you care about
- The meaning of your time here on earth
- The goals you want to achieve
- The work you want to invest yourself in

Be grateful – Go against the grain and choose to bring continued, hopeful, and expectant attention to your world. Complaining is a waste of your time.

Bored, anxious, restless, or uninspired? Take steps to connect more fully with your world. Up the challenge. Make things matter. Be present, even in the mundane things. Life becomes meaningful when you overcome adversity or achieve a goal—so expect more of yourself. Have a rock-solid WHY and live on purpose.

Remember the Serenity Prayer and engrave it on your soul:

"God, grant me the serenity to accept the things I cannot change, the courage to change the things I can, and the wisdom to know the difference."

Strive for wisdom, discernment, and self-honesty. From the moment you wake up, tension will start to accumulate. At the end of every day, take the time to just let it all go.

Toxic positivity will only increase the power that negativity has over you. Instead, practice negative visualization, look fear and discomfort straight in the eyes, and toughen up. Life can be hard. But it's way harder when you're enslaved by self-deception, excuses, low expectations, passivity, distraction, and avoidance.

Don't be surprised by adversity or disappointment. Be prepared for it.

Respond to noise and distraction with indifference and always remember that you don't have to respond at all. You don't have to care, and you don't have to have an opinion.

Composure is about constant course-correction.

Stay on top of everyday tensions with calming micro-activities. Slow down, get outside, have a real conversation. Check in frequently and adjust yourself—catch minor disturbances before they become major ones.

Take control and be ruthless with clutter, digital noise, and distraction. Commit to protecting your mind from overstimulation. Take things at your own pace and learn to simplify your routines, your daily habits, and your decision-making process.

Peace is simplicity. Complexity is stressful.

Don't burn yourself out doing something that doesn't need to be done.

Fear is the most bothersome emotion. Reconsider your relationship to it.

Healthy fear protects.

Unhealthy fear restricts.

Remember that a fearful response to fear only reinforces that fear. Instead of escape and avoidance, face your limiting fear and get to know it. Talk to it. Treat it like the inconsequential house guest it is.

Don't wait until you feel brave! You can live a rich, meaningful life even though you experience anxiety, self-doubt, or low confidence. You can take action even though you're afraid.

Fear is a fact of life, but when you commit to taking small steps in the right direction, fear doesn't have a hold of you anymore—you have a hold of it.

Name your fear and step outside of it. Get that distance. Take a breath.

Tell yourself: "Fear is just a sensation."

You've survived it before and you'll survive it again. Stand tall literally and you will feel taller and firmer *mentally*. Be honest about the fear crutches you're using and demand better for yourself—learning that you are so much stronger than you thought is one of the best gifts you can hope to receive.

Don't be disturbed by noise, chaos, and drama.

Tune into the signal, ignore the noise. Use your brainpower to chart a path to your purpose, not to process endless overstimulation. Care, but care wisely.

Even the most painful or embarrassing criticism holds a gem for us if we're willing to pause and reflect. As long as we frame other people's statements, opinions, judgments, and claims as *simple data*, we will cease to be emotionally bothered by them.

Finally, own your power to just *stop bothering yourself*. Just because you thought something, doesn't mean you have to take your own word for it!

Thoughts are not facts or commands, and they're not permanent.

Don't get hooked by them. Instead, become aware and label them without judgment or interpretation. Self-distance and reappraise with a fresh perspective.

The things of life can come and go—your job is to grab hold of what's good, and let the rest just pass you by. It's not yours. It doesn't deserve any space in your head. Don't help it bother you.

Zoom out and watch quietly from afar.

Confucius said, **"The noble-minded are calm and steady. Little people are forever fussing and fretting."**

Forget about the fretting and fussing. Set your intention on becoming noble-minded.

www.ingramcontent.com/pod-product-compliance
Lightning Source LLC
Chambersburg PA
CBHW022221090526
44585CB00013BB/660